D0560595

ADVANCE PRAISE FOR
CHANGE THE WAY YOU CHANGE!

"Leaders, take notice . . . In leadership, what worked yesterday won't work today. *Change the Way You Change!* outlines a fresh, inside-out approach for getting better results in the twenty-first century."

—Doug Conant, founder and CEO of ConantLeadership
and former CEO of Campbell Soup Company

"In my ten years of working with Tony and Kendall at two companies, I've found them to be highly insightful organization effectiveness consultants who can quickly diagnose a suboptimal situation and provide very practical guidance and tools that can help executives and teams dramatically improve their performance. They are keen students of human behavior and executive leadership and have amassed an encyclopedic knowledge of how modern theories of management and frameworks for organization development can be applied to the real issues that impede teamwork and results. Based on their cumulative learnings from engagements with hundreds of executives in many different industries, *Change the Way You Change!* is an invaluable resource for anyone seeking to secure the next level of success in change for themselves, as executives, their team, and their company."

—Chip Perry, CEO of TrueCar Incorporated
and former CEO of AutoTrader.com

"The first challenge in any change effort is getting our leadership team fully committed to the future vision, and too often we find ourselves "getting the results that we are perfectly designed to get." Kendall and Tony have gone beyond the ADKAR model with a practical framework and real-world examples that get to the heart of change management. From chartering and alignment to keeping score and building accountability, *Change The Way You Change* provides exactly what is required to confidently transform your business for the better."

—Douglas R. Guthrie, senior vice president of Comcast

"With everything going on in the world today, this extraordinary book, *Change the Way You Change!*, comes to us at a perfect time. Tony and Kendall have written a masterpiece that is both deeply thought-provoking and practical. If you want to accelerate your inner game and are passionate about becoming a more effective leader, then buckle up . . . you are in for a real treat!"

—Tom Mitchell PhD, coauthor of *The Winning Spirit*
(with NFL Hall of Famer, Joe Montana)

"In reading *Change The Way You Change!*, I kept finding myself saying: 'With this information, we can immediately enhance our own model of change!' For years now, I've wanted to create an ultra-high-end level of service for families needing to change. Believe it or not, this book maps out the principles for doing just that. Obviously sharing their best stuff, this blueprint isn't only impressive, it's entertaining. There is no way some less capable and experienced change experts could distill this kind of information in a way that the reader can apply it to bring about organizational change. True experts and years and years of experience are required. I'll be quoting from this book for years to come."

—Tim Thayne, PhD, founder and CEO Homeward Bound, and author of *Not by Chance: How Parents Boost Their Teen's Success In and After Treatment*

"This book is a fit traveling companion for those embarking on organizational change. It shows you not only where the quicksand is but also where and how to accelerate the process. All of my experience confirms Kendall and Tony's premise that successful change leaders must focus on three units of performance—the individual, the team, and the organization. Change leadership must and always will be tactical and strategic, gritty and conceptual, directive and collaborative, and realistic and idealistic. Leading change is the supreme test of the leader, and this book is the distilled wisdom of two masters of the craft."

—Timothy R. Clark, CEO, LeaderFactor, author of
Epic Change: How to Lead Change in the Global Age

"*Change the Way You Change* is a tour de force. The five leader activities (focus, align, engage, lead, and sustain) capture the change landscape. The tools and tips turn the ideas into actions for anyone who deals with change (who is everyone in today's world). Bravo!"

—Dave Ulrich, Rensis Likert, professor at Ross School of Business,
University of Michigan; partner, the RBL Group

"Kendall and Tony have written an insightful how-to book for anyone seriously considering initiating real change within their organization. While there are no silver bullets for implementing transformational change, *Change the Way You Change!* provides the reader with plenty of ammunition to help him or her as they lead their organization in the change battle. Kendall and Tony have brought together, in one place, the key insights and truths they have learned from years of experience helping leaders implement meaningful and effective change."

—Major General Craig Bambrough, United States Army (retired)

"Kendall and Tony's outstanding book crystalizes the reality that the leader is the catalyst for change and the engine for success. The insights provided in their book can help leaders become productive agents for changing the culture, the performance, and the fundamental nature of an organization. It's a must read for anyone charged with the responsibility of leading an organization in today's dynamic environment."

—John Aplin, managing director at CID Capital

"As seasoned vets in the field of change, Kendall and Tony have an unparalleled ability to logically translate the essentials of transformation. Every quote, story, example, and concept in *Change the Way You Change!* will resonate in a way that will enable you to reflect, review, and expand your change capabilities in the moments that matter. If you're truly interested in transformation, take the time to internalize, adapt, and apply. This book has masterfully articulated the stuff that actually works!"

—Lisa Strogal, former manager of culture, change,
and talent at Cenovus Energy

"As president and founder of the Woman's Presidents Association, we have deep leadership conversations with literally hundreds of our highly successful woman-owned businesses around the world. Change in business is a ticket to admission in today's fast-paced economy and especially for small to medium-size businesses. In their book, *Change the Way You Change!*, Lyman and Daloisio have captured the essence of highly effective leadership of change in business. The style and substance of this book are spot on for my members, and I will highly recommend it to them to read, study, and apply to accelerate change and achieve the goals in their business."

—Marsha Firestone, president and founder
of Woman's Presidents Association

"This book hits the nail on the head. Leading effective change demands that you make very wise choices due to limited resources, strong competition, and a dynamic marketplace. Tony and Kendall have put their career experience, hard earned life lessons, and spirited personalities into your hands with this book."

—Matthew J. Claus, principal, Claus Advisory Group, LLC

"In *Change the Way You Change!*, Kendall and Tony provide an arsenal of tools to successfully lead change. As important, they transform the reader's apprehension about the prospect of change to an enthusiasm to drive it."

—Mike Sherman, president and CEO, Endocyte, Incorporated

"The challenge in a book on transformation is to get the balance right between conceptual framing and practical tools for application. Kendall and Tony got it right. The five roles of effective leaders are spot on to what it takes to make things happen."

—Norm Smallwood, cofounder of the RBL Group

"*Change the Way You Change!* captures the essence of the experienced practitioner . . . a field guide to the challenges, concepts, and realities of being a leader of significant change. Across all industries, sectors, and geographies, the lessons provided by Tony and Kendall capture what it really takes to lead change."

—Richard Maltsbarger, chief development officer and president, international of Lowe's Companies, Incorporated

"Is there a fast track to change? Yes—when you lead inside out *and* outside in. The challenge is that you have to do more than talk about change; you must become it. Tony and Kendall are authorities on this approach because they do more than explain the inside-out work—they live it."

—Mette Norgaard, coauthor of *TouchPoints* and
author of *The Ugly Duckling Goes to Work*

"*Change the Way You Change!* is an incredible handbook that helps leaders navigate and accelerate change in these turbulent times. It provides in-depth insight into leading change rather than managing change to truly accelerate the transformation. Reading this book will enable one to better lead a change process. It is a must read for change leaders at all levels."

—Patricia W. Longshore, vice president,
strategic leadership solutions, Duke Corporate Education

"*Change the Way You Change!* is a leadership book that is neither too academic for practitioners nor too shallow for academic audiences. It is just right for anyone who is curious about accelerating change leadership. It provides an approach to change leadership efforts and builds a strong case for the necessity of simultaneously working at the individual, team, and organizational levels to successfully navigate the speed and complexity of change. The systems level approach presents five roles that are not just old wine in new bottles."

—Terry C. Blum, professor and director, Institute for Leadership and
Entrepreneurship, Scheller College of Business, Georgia Tech

"Leaders in companies, nonprofits, and governments all understand the urgent need to change the way their organizations operate to remain competitive and in some cases to survive. *Change The Way You Change!* is a practical guide to help leaders clearly identify, kick-start, and then sustain change campaigns within their organizations. With clear, straightforward writing peppered with real-world examples, the book offers step-by-step planning tools, checklists for implementation, and warning signs that a derailment may be approaching. Daloisio and Lyman, whose life work has focused on the successful implementation of change management strategies across a broad range of industries, clearly understand the pain that results for leaders who can't get their organizations to change or change fast enough. In this book, they unselfishly reveal their most successful strategies and tactics for faster, more effective change initiatives. As a lawyer representing high-growth companies, entrepreneurs and nonprofits for more than two decades, I can't think of a single leader, myself included, who wouldn't benefit from reading *Change the Way You Change!*"

—**Mary Donne Peters, author, speaker, and cofounder Gorby Peters Law**

"Contemplating organizational change is perhaps one of the most daunting tasks for any organizational leader. While the company's performance indicators may scream for change, a walk through the graveyard of failed change efforts causes all but the most courageous to hide and hope for the best. In their very accessible and practical book, Kendall Lyman and Tony Daloisio provide strategies, stories, and thought-provoking questions, so that leaders can take heart and master the process of change. The core message is that mastering change is a holistic and simultaneous inside-out and outside-in process, which ensures harmonization of vision and elegance of execution. Lyman and Daloisio also remind leaders that organizational change cannot happen unless they change as well. Because the authors are true experts in this work, their proposed steps for action are tried and tested. Their examples demonstrate that the approach can work for both microenterprises as well as huge conglomerates while also providing a roadmap for personal growth and organizational transformation. A good read!"

—Catharyn Baird, founder and CEO of EthicsGame

"Tony and Kendall have provided an essential roadmap for anyone who wants to lead or influence change in their organization. Read this and get started!"

—Alan Fine, founder and president of InsideOut Development

"*Change the Way You Change!* is a great book for managers who want to improve their organization's results. It's full of practical ideas and useful tools that Kendall and Tony bring to life with countless stories from their personal experiences in the trenches with their clients. It also has crisp summaries at the end of each chapter and the end of the book that make it easy to remember the key points and go back to find a topic you're looking for. If you want to know the right questions to ask in order to make your next change initiative successful, this is a must read!"

—**John Beck, Principle Charter Oak Consulting Group**
and author of *The Leaders Window*

"A great read full of practical tips and profound wisdom for understanding and driving the complexity of organizational change. Lyman and Daloisio have crafted a comprehensive guide for navigating the treacherous seas of change so essential to organizational viability in the twenty-first century. Their advice comes from decades of experience partnering with leaders of some of the most prestigious companies in the world. If you are responsible for leading change or want to distinguish yourself as a change agent who can 'make it stick,' you should buy and use this book."

—**Neil Yeager, coauthor of** *The Leader's Window,* **the best-selling** *Power Interviews,* **and** *The Seventh Prism*

CHANGE!

THE WAY YOU CHANGE

5 ROLES OF LEADERS
WHO ACCELERATE
BUSINESS PERFORMANCE

R. KENDALL LYMAN AND
TONY C. DALOISIO

GREENLEAF
BOOK GROUP PRESS

This publication is designed to provide accurate and authoritative information in regard to the subject matter covered. It is sold with the understanding that the publisher and author are not engaged in rendering legal, accounting, or other professional services. If legal advice or other expert assistance is required, the services of a competent professional should be sought.

Published by Greenleaf Book Group Press
Austin, Texas
www.gbgpress.com

Copyright ©2017 R. Kendall Lyman and Tony C. Daloisio

All rights reserved.

Thank you for purchasing an authorized edition of this book and for complying with copyright law. No part of this book may be reproduced, stored in a retrieval system, or transmitted by any means, electronic, mechanical, photocopying, recording, or otherwise, without written permission from the copyright holder.

Distributed by Greenleaf Book Group

For ordering information or special discounts for bulk purchases, please contact Greenleaf Book Group at PO Box 91869, Austin, TX 78709, 512.891.6100.

Design and composition by Greenleaf Book Group and Kim Lance
Cover design by Greenleaf Book Group and Kim Lance
Cover image ©Spantomoda/Thinkstock.com

Cataloging-in-Publication data is available.

Print ISBN: 978-1-62634-417-4

eBook ISBN: 978-1-62634-418-1

Part of the Tree Neutral® program, which offsets the number of trees consumed in the production and printing of this book by taking proactive steps, such as planting trees in direct proportion to the number of trees used: www.treeneutral.com

Tree Neutral

Printed in the United States of America on acid-free paper

17 18 19 20 21 22   10 9 8 7 6 5 4 3 2 1

First Edition

To our clients who have given us their trust and the opportunity to create and refine these ideas and practices.

CONTENTS

FOREWORD

Heraclitus, the Greek philosopher-general, famously stated that "the only constant is change." I believe he was only partially right. I prefer the more comprehensive perspective my late father, Dr. Stephen R. Covey, used to teach that there are indeed *three* constants: 1) change, 2) principles, and 3) choice.

In today's global marketplace, change is accelerating as a constant. Political systems, consumer preferences, shifting demographics, global market conditions, and new and disruptive technologies are upending established organizations and time-tested approaches. For leaders, it can be overwhelming.

As a CEO, I experienced this firsthand at Covey Leadership Center, the company founded by my father. When I became president and CEO in 1994, we had a company that had been well-led but was undermanaged. Clients loved us, we had great content and solutions, and were growing rapidly (perhaps too rapidly). While we had a great value proposition for our clients, we hadn't yet figured out a sustainable business model for ourselves. We had had 11 straight years of negative cash flow, had very low operating margins, had a lot of debt, had no outside capital, and had high growth. Do the math on that—we were going to run out of cash! We had nearly gone bankrupt twice, had suppliers who were ready to quit on us, and our debt to equity ratio (as measured by our bank in the form of Total Liabilities to Tangible Net Worth) was 223:1! It wasn't due to malfeasance or bad intent—we just hadn't yet figured out a sustainable business model and a major contributor for our challenges was the lack of accurate accounting. In short, however, it was untenable.

Within three years, we righted the company by *choosing* to follow enduring *principles* in the face of all the *changes* that were happening to us and that we needed to make for us to continue our mission of taking enduring principles to the world. During that period, the company's sales nearly doubled and profit went up over 1,200 percent. The company expanded into 40 different countries and we increased shareholder value from $2.4 million to $160 million in a merger we orchestrated with then Franklin Quest to form a new company called FranklinCovey. This turnaround tale isn't about me; instead, it creates the context and highlights several choices based upon principles we deeply validated through this process.

First, surround yourself with great leaders and trust them to deliver results. Increasing the collective capacity of leaders is a critical investment for meaningful change. Second, make the creation of trust with your stakeholders an explicit objective—indeed, an organizational imperative. Without trust, organizations and leaders experience a tax or burden on everything they do—everything takes you longer to do and costs you more; by contrast, with trust, barriers come down and performance improves—everything happens faster and at far less cost. And third, to create change, leaders must help employees transition and align the organization to facilitate those transitions. Each of these approaches by themselves is necessary—but they are individually insufficient for lasting success.

This is why I'm excited about this terrific book *Change the Way You Change!* Tony and Kendall have succinctly captured many lessons I have learned as a leader of change, and it mirrors my experience helping clients build trust in themselves, in their various stakeholder relationships, and in their organizations.

The great historian Arnold Toynbee studied the rise and fall of civilizations over time. When asked to describe his life's work, he simply said: "I can do it in four words: *Nothing fails like success*." This is a lesson that is first learned and later earned. We *learned* this lesson first from clients. It wasn't that we failed with clients, but over and over again in workshops and engagements around the world they told us that personal improvement stagnates when it bumps up against an ineffective team climate and misaligned organizational processes and systems. So we brought in Tony Daloisio, who was simply indispensable to helping us develop a consulting practice at Covey Leadership Center that leveraged our work with individuals in the classroom to the work that needed to be done with leaders in the boardroom.

After learning from clients, we really *earned* our understanding of Toynbee's insights through the merger between Franklin Quest and the Covey Leadership Center. What we thought would be an "easy" marriage of two great companies given the proximity of headquarters, demographics of employees, and similarity in values was in reality challenging and at times incredibly frustrating as employees struggled with issues we hadn't anticipated both at the individual and organizational levels. Kendall Lyman helped us navigate the merger successfully and later became the leader of our organizational change practice. Together with other skilled practitioners, Tony and Kendall applied what we had learned internally to our clients' issues with amazing success.

Leading change wisely is even more important today than when we were growing FranklinCovey—in fact, it's a non-negotiable imperative for leaders. For many leaders, leading change is a slippery slope that dashes their best intentions and careers because they either take it on piecemeal or don't have a clear understanding of how to change an organization systemically. That's a risky proposition for leadership success and longevity! Consequently, many leaders dabble at the edges of change or avoid it altogether. This book can transform how you lead change for three important reasons: the approach works, it shows you what to do, and it's immediately applicable.

First, the current approach to leading change is typically incomplete. From my own work in helping leaders build trust, results only sustainably improve when individuals become credible, behaviors change to improve relationships and team dynamics, organizations align to create an environment where trust flourishes, and influence is extended into markets and societies. Too many leaders want to only work at one or two levels. But lasting success comes when you focus your efforts on *all* of these areas. What we discovered as we helped organizations and took our own medicine internally (so to speak) is that change is *both* an inside-out quest as well as an outside-in process. This is not only a change in thinking, but also requires an overhaul to how leaders approach change.

Second, in this book Tony and Kendall show what it takes for leaders to successfully lead change. Leaders must be the champions of the change focus, the architects of the organization, the coach that engages employee passion, and the student of leadership focused on improving their capabilities and the collective leadership capabilities of the organization. This book does an amazing job teaching leaders all the roles they must play to be successful in change.

And third, Tony and Kendall have struck a beautiful balance in this book between leadership imperatives and practical frontline execution principles. This approach works—it has been tested in the trenches and refined through continued application. Whether you lead a project team or a major organization, applying the principles in this book will be a tipping point to success in your change effort.

As one who has known and worked with Kendall and Tony for over 20 years, I highly recommend this wonderful book! Having worked closely with them through the years on client engagements, research, and methodology, I know they are both persons of complete integrity who care about people. They are truly trusted advisors of great insight, skill, and perspective. I'm confident this book will become one of your favorites not only for you but for your key leaders and managers as well.

If you're ready to lead a performance improvement in your team or organization, this remarkable book will help you change the way you change. And by changing the way *you* change, you will create the trust and results needed in your world. And when you get results in a way that inspires trust, anything is possible.

—Stephen M. R. Covey, December 6, 2016

INTRODUCTION

What do you know about change? How do you know if you're successful at leading change? Because of the rapidly changing pace of the business world, leading change has become as integral to a leader's success as managing the balance sheet or implementing a new customer service program. Yet research indicates that less than 30% of change efforts succeed. Why?

Most leaders lack a complete picture of how change happens. Too many continue to tinker with tactics and short-term fixes while hoping for transformation and long-term improvement. Many leaders ask others to engage and change without really understanding how to do that themselves. All too often leaders are rewarded for doing their "day job," so they haphazardly lead change "on the side." This results in change feeling fragmented, complicated, or theoretical by those on the front line—those who are required to implement the change.

The current approach to change is incomplete. Until leaders adopt a new approach, their results will be elusive, left to chance, and doomed to similar low success rates. In addition, change fatigue and employee skepticism will increase, reducing the chance for sustainable change and real competitive advantage. Great leaders of change positively impact business performance by fundamentally working differently from most leaders in three ways. First, they change how they think and talk about change. Second, they change their approach to change by engaging both individuals *and* the organization. And third, they elevate what they do as a leader and the roles they play.

In any other profession, a 70% failure rate would be unacceptable. It's time we make it so in the professional ranks of leadership.

Voters, boards of directors, employees, and customers are all scream-
ing for change. If they are not in your industry, they soon will be. The
only way to survive as a leader in the twenty-first century is to make
change part of your leadership agenda. And that means making it a
priority and getting good at it.

The intent of this book is to help leaders evolve what they know
about change so that they can transform their leadership and their
business. This book provides a "how to" approach that will help anyone champion change no matter their role, organization, or industry. It gives a common language and set of tools to help teams get
on the same page, align their work, and collaborate to get faster and
better results.

This approach works. It has been tested over the past twenty-five
years. It is practical and can be replicated. Whether you are a begin-
ner or an expert, this book shows you how to attain deep and lasting change. In short, this approach will help you *change the way you
change* to accelerate your leadership and results.

1

CHANGE THE WAY YOU CHANGE!

"There is nothing more difficult to carry out, nor more doubtful of success, nor more dangerous to handle than to initiate a new order of things. For the reformer has enemies in all those who profit by the old order, and only lukewarm defenders by all those who could profit by the new order. This lukewarmness arises from the incredulity of mankind who do not truly believe in anything new until they have had actual experiences with it."

–Niccolo Machiavelli, Italian historian, politician, diplomat, philosopher, and writer

O n a blustery November evening many years ago, Gay Hendricks (a psychologist and writer) was obliged to go to a party he didn't want to attend. You know the kind—where you are expected to plaster a smile on your face, meet people you're not interested in, and make small talk about subjects that seemingly have no real purpose. In his own words he said, "We'd been to the party about an hour, and I was dutifully shuffling around from one guest to another. I'd just about given up trying to be convivial when I was introduced to a tall fellow named Ed. His restless fidgeting suggested that he was having about as much fun as I was. I mentioned this to him, and he endeared himself to me by saying, 'I loathe parties—can't stand the small talk.'"

So the two of them changed the conversation and entered into what they called "Big Talk." Gay Hendricks said the conversation "changed my life." He went on to write a book called *Five Wishes* that further explored his conversation that night.

In our experience working with leaders, we've found the conversations (and consequently the actions) about change to be of the same quality as those at an obligatory party—small talk. Very few leaders are having Big Talk conversations about change that are transforming lives and impacting results. Very few are engaging in conversations that address questions such as these:

- How effective are we at delivering results?

- What do we need to do to increase our performance capacity?

- What needs to happen that is not happening now?

- What pain are we experiencing now in the business?

- What is it costing the organization to have this problem?

- If we were to start with a clean slate, what would we do differently?

- How effective are we as leaders? How do we know?

- In our organizational culture, what is the level of commitment to change and improve performance?

- How effective are we at having leadership conversations that enable us to creatively solve business challenges?

- What, if anything, might prevent the organization from successfully implementing change?[1]

Instead of grappling with Big Talk questions like those listed, we usually see leaders cautiously creep along the following continuum:

Postpone → Passively Approach → Piecemeal

- **Postpone**: Leaders who postpone change have multiple reasons. They may be in their role for only a short time, so why start something they can't finish? Or they might rationalize that because the volume of change is so great, it's better to change later—it's almost too much to deal with now. So they go on a change diet where they cut out anything that might upset the status quo.

- **Passively Approach**: Leaders who passively approach change never quite get down to the heart of it. They circle round, stand at the edges, maybe let a little sink in, but they don't embrace it for themselves or champion it for others. These leaders talk the good change talk, but there is no action. Their communication lands in the ears of employees like *small* talk because no *big* change ever occurs.

- **Piecemeal**: Leaders who use a piecemeal approach to change work on a system here or a process there, but they fail to realize the holistic nature of change. They try out a lot of small improvements, but those changes typically yield small results. They rarely tackle the tough work of transforming the business, improving the customer experience, or aligning priorities.

Instead of these small-change approaches, the only sustainable approach is one that is proactive. Proactive leaders understand that to create long-term, sustainable improvements they must step into wholesale change—approaching it from all angles. The proactive approach is not only a calculated move to improve results, it is also a way to engage in Big Talk conversations with key stakeholders—an important component of generating ideas for better results.

Where are you on the continuum of change? Are you talking big but playing small? Or are you engaging others in the difficult questions about change and then proactively executing the work that needs to be done? General Eric Shinseki (Ret.), US Army Chief of Staff, said, "If you don't like change, you're going to like irrelevance even less." Today, anything but the proactive approach will get you swept away by the "whitewater" of change to irrelevance. At cocktail parties, you can afford small talk. At the office, Big Talk is the only real conversation that will keep you relevant. And to remain relevant, you must grow, adapt, and change.

...

"One does not discover new lands without consenting to lose sight of the shore for a very long time."

—Andre Gide, French novelist

WHAT IS AND ISN'T WORKING WITH CHANGE?

If you have led a change initiative and were to do it again, what would you emphasize and what would you avoid? That's the journey that we have been on for the last twenty-five years—figuring out what works and what doesn't in the change process by helping leaders who struggle with the constancy of change in business environments that have grown increasingly complex. Here is what we've found:

1. **Lackluster Results**: Leaders and employees alike are disappointed and disillusioned by change and less than satisfied with results. If, as studies have shown, only 30% of change efforts are a success, it's no wonder contemplating change breeds frustration and an unwillingness to keep trying. To many, it feels like leaders aren't learning from failures and don't know how to repeat successes in the future.

2. **Lack of Leadership**: Change initiatives continue to lack the buy-in from employees and support from cross-functional team leaders. Too often the change approach doesn't quite fit the situation, or there is a feeling of "here we go again." In a 2014 study that asked, *What has been the single greatest contributor to the success of your change management program?* active and visible sponsorship was listed as number one. (In fact, it was cited over three times more frequently than the next contributor.)[2] The study found that effective leaders of change were almost 3.5 times more likely to meet or exceed project objectives than were their ineffective counterparts. Great change leaders actively guide their organizations through transitions while enabling individuals and teams to engage in the changes.

3. **Incomplete Approach**: Too many leaders have an incomplete picture of how change happens. Current change literature and practitioners advocate a one-dimensional approach to change that doesn't yield long-term results. One approach focuses on changing individuals to enable them to change so that they can change their environment. Another approach works on organizational processes and systems with the intent of fostering a change in individual behavior. But a one-dimensional approach doesn't lead to sustainable change. Either employees will break themselves against business practices that haven't changed, or

the lack of aligned systems will confuse employee priorities. For change to stick, it must deal with emotions and employee transitions *and* improve the effectiveness of how the business is run. Sustainable change only happens when individual, team, and organizational transformations happen concurrently.

4. **Success Breeds Success**: A team's confidence in its ability to lead change increases once they have seen and experienced a practical approach to change. If leaders want different results than they've had in the past, they have to do things differently than they've ever done them before. But most leaders (and teams) don't know what that looks like. The application of change principles, success practices, and tools doesn't have to follow a smorgasbord approach to change where leaders try "some of this and some of that" or use "one of these and one of those" best practices. These approaches fail because they don't apply ideas consistently or holistically. A practical approach to change is just that—something that can be applied easily at any level of the organization to enable change and improve performance. In one study, almost 50% of participants believed that at least half of the resistance to change they experienced could have been avoided with better change management.[3]

5. **Leadership Is Level Agnostic**: Successful leaders of change enable everyone in the organization to be a champion of change. Hoping employees engage in change engenders an attitude of watching a parade vs. actively participating in it. Hope is not a strategy. The speed and complexity of change are increasing, and high-performing organizations don't have the time to deal with those who are not engaged and contributing (see Appendix 1: The Complexity and Speed of Change). All of us are part of a team that either runs something, makes something, or recommends something. In that role—whether we are the leader or a team member—we're all expected to make

it better, improve how we work, or get better results. One finding indicated that 60% of the participants surveyed didn't feel their organization did an adequate job preparing managers to lead change.[4] We have found that to be consistent across all levels within organizations. With change becoming more complicated, all employees must learn to champion it.

CHANGING HOW CHANGE HAPPENS: THREE THINGS THAT GREAT LEADERS OF CHANGE DO DIFFERENTLY

The first thing that great leaders of change do differently is change how they think and talk about change. They engage in Big Talk—conversations about the business that proactively explore sustainable improvements through wholesale change. This is what we discussed at the beginning of the chapter.

The second thing great leaders of change do is change their approach to change by engaging both individuals *and* the organization in change. In almost every book we read about change, the authors start with a premise about how change happens. And yet they rarely agree. Here are some examples:

- "Changing the system will change what people do. Changing what people do will not change the system."[5]

- "You simply cannot get the results you need without getting into 'that personal stuff.' The results depend on getting people to stop doing things the old way and getting them to start doing things a new way. There is no way to do that impersonally."[6]

Some authors (and many change practitioners) argue that change starts with individuals. Others claim that individuals can't really change until the organization does. These premises led us to ask,

"How does change happen? Does change happen from the inside-out or from the outside-in?" In other words, is the most effective way to change an organization accomplished by helping individuals change so they, in turn, can change their teams and the organization (inside-out)? Or is the best approach to improve the organizational elements of strategy, processes, and structure, and then expect teams and individual behavior to align with the changes so as to deliver better results (outside-in)? The difference is summarized in the table below:

Inside-Out Approach to Change	Outside-In Approach to Change
Emphasis: Focus on enabling individuals to change first.	**Emphasis:** Focus on enabling the organization to change first.
Philosophers of this school of change emphasize: "Teach a man to fish, and he will fish for a lifetime."	**Philosophers of this school of change emphasize:** "Form follows function, and function follows strategy."
Representative Quote: "Discover a few vital behaviors, change those, and problems—no matter their size—topple like a house of cards."[7]	**Representative Quote:** "The problem is, how do you develop an environment in which individuals can be creative? I believe that you have to put a good deal of thought to your organizational structure in order to provide this environment."[8]
The Process of Change: Starts with changing individual behaviors; translating those to team goals, measures, and behaviors; and then aligning the organizational processes, structure, and support systems to enable the behaviors and results.	**The Process of Change:** Starts with getting clear about the strategy, vision, and purpose of the organization; then aligning the organizational processes, structure, and support systems to deliver on the new strategic priorities; then translating the strategy to team goals and measures; and ultimately creating individual scorecards and behaviors to clarify what individuals do to implement the strategy.

So which change approach do you subscribe to? When you lead change, do you start with getting clear about the desired individual behaviors and then align the organization to reinforce those behaviors? Or do you start by getting clear about the focus of the organization and then getting people on board? It's hard to choose one or the other, isn't it? They both seem like solid, logical ways to change.

So we asked ourselves: does it have to be either/or? We engaged in change endeavors with clients, watched, and used both approaches. Over and over we wondered: does it have to be either/or?

After many years of considering this question, we have found the answer is "no." In fact, for change to be sustainable, our answer is a resounding *no*! Even though it hasn't been written about a great deal, here's the truth as we know it: *lasting change requires both an inside-out and an outside-in approach.* It *has to.* How many times have you seen change fail because it started at the top but fizzled out by the time it got down to employees? Or your organization sent employees to a workshop and they got excited about personal improvement, only to go back to their jobs and run up against the processes, structures, or policies that were not aligned with their new, changed behavior? Robert Pirsig described it well when he said the following:

> If a factory is torn down but the rationality which produced it is left standing, then the rationality will simply produce another factory. If a revolution destroys a systematic government, but the systematic patterns of thought that produced that government are left intact, then those patterns will repeat themselves in the succeeding government.[9]

In short, to change a team or business, you have to change both the thoughts and beliefs *and* the structure and systems. And to get it to stick, all levels of the organization have to be focused, aligned, and engaged on the same thing—and that takes leadership! Great leaders of change engage both individuals *and* the organization. We call this inside-out and outside-in change. For change to be successful, it must include both outside-in and inside-out efforts that become the two key elements of a reinforcing loop.

...

"Organizational change, when you get right down to it, boils down to persuading massive numbers of people to stop doing what they've been doing for years and to start doing something they probably don't want to do—at least not at first."

—David Nadler, leadership consultant and author

Think of a change you were involved in, either personally or professionally, that was successful. Likely your success with change included the following elements:

- A clear dissatisfaction or discomfort with the current state

- A clear vision of the future describing how it would look and feel

- A plan to improve performance

- An alignment of the processes, structure, and systems designed to achieve the vision

- Clear steps to enable greater collaboration between leaders and teams

- A plan to increase the engagement, capacity, and capability of people in the organization

- A plan to improve the individual skills required to implement the change

If you think about the successes, you will likely see a pattern of both outside-in and inside-out efforts going on simultaneously. Together these reinforce each other to create improved results.

On the other hand, we have watched campaigns of change full of important speeches, fancy slogans and promises, and music blaring from the bandstands that ultimately went nowhere and produced very few tangible results. These failures likely included attempts at either outside-in or inside-out change, but didn't address both. The cost of poor change leadership is staggering and often leads to the following:

- A low sense of urgency

- Little understanding about the reasons for change

- A lack of commitment and action from frontline employees who ask, "What's in it for me?"

- Organizational obstacles obstructing the path of implementation

- A culture and organization architecture that inhibits rather than enables behavior change

If you think about change failures, you'll likely see leaders not working at all three levels of the organization.

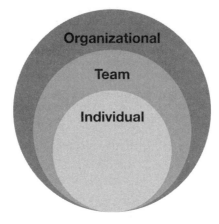

Diagram: Three Levels of Change

Working at the organizational level includes setting direction, clarifying structural roles and responsibilities, aligning processes and systems, and creating a culture of shared beliefs and norms. Executives and boards most often drive outside-in efforts based on changes in the external environment and strategic goals.

Leaders who mainly work at the organizational level must also address the behaviors and culture of the organization. This can't be a "quick fix" that changes the structure or merely mandates new policies. As one change practitioner, Michael Hammer, said, "Coming up with the ideas [for change] is the easy part, but getting things done is the tough part. The place where these reforms die is . . . down in the trenches."[10] Warning: A weak attempt at outside-in change, such as moving lines and boxes on the org chart, is analogous to rearranging chairs on the *Titanic*. Ultimately, the result will be the same because no significant action has been taken to fix the underlying problems. Outside-in approaches are necessary but insufficient to improve organization results.

...

**"The world fears a new experience more than it fears anything.
Because a new experience displaces so many old experiences....
The world doesn't fear a new idea. It can pigeon-hole any idea. But
it can't pigeon-hole a new experience."**

—D. H. Lawrence, British novelist

Working effectively at the individual and team level begins with frontline, customer-facing employees. If change is not focused on getting the commitment, ownership, and buy-in of all employees—top to bottom—it will fail. Effective change leaders know that their role is to help employees move along an individual continuum of change.

UNAWARENESS → AWARENESS → UNDERSTANDING → ACCEPTANCE → COMMITMENT

- **Unawareness:** Employees don't know that a change is happening.

- **Awareness:** Employees are aware things are changing, but don't know what, why, when, or how.

- **Understanding:** Employees logically understand the change, but don't yet believe it will impact them.

- **Acceptance:** Employees accept that the changes will impact them, and they begin adapting accordingly.

- **Commitment:** Employees embrace the change and willingly alter their behavior in support of it.

To enable the movement along the individual change continuum, great change leaders engage the heads, the hands, and the hearts of their employees:

- They engage the HEAD of each employee with facts, logic, rationale, data, and strategic plans.

- They engage the HANDS of employees by letting them try out the change, determine if the changes are reliable, get involved in fixing problems, and link the changes to the work they will do day in and day out in their teams.

- They engage the HEART of their people through stories of success, a vision for the future, empowerment in the now, and engagement and passion for the potential promised by the change.

Inside-out approaches are critical to success, but also insufficient to achieve sustainable results. When both an outside-in and an inside-out approach to change are combined, employees become engaged in change.

Research shows that organizations with highly engaged employees outperform rivals in operating income by 19%, net income by 14%, and earnings per share by 28%.[11] Unless employees are on board "down in the trenches," leaders will struggle with implementation. It's critical that change leaders get both the technical solution right (outside-in) and help other leaders, managers, and employees want it (inside-out). When employees are committed to change and the organization is aligned to reinforce that commitment, transformations are accelerated. Sustainable change only happens when individual, team, and organizational transformation happen concurrently.

...

"There is no contest between the company that buys the grudging compliance of its work force and the company that enjoys the enterprising participation of its employees."

—Ricardo Semler, author, CEO of Semco SA

Quick-fix changes don't work to improve our own personal health, and similarly they don't work to improve long-term organizational health. To get lasting personal health improvements, we need to focus on nutrition, exercise, sleep, and stress reduction. To get lasting organizational health improvements, leaders need to create a culture that delivers lasting results. And that includes setting the direction, enabling processes and systems to work effectively, getting buy-in from employees, and "walking the talk." When all of these elements come together, change will happen at all levels.

The third thing that great change leaders do differently from most leaders is elevate the roles they play. Booker T. Washington said, "Success is to be measured not so much by the position that one has reached in life as by the obstacles which he has overcome." With change becoming more complex, leaders must adopt new roles to enable the organization to find solutions to the new realities and obstacles of the business. There are five roles that great change leaders play to successfully lead change from the outside-in and inside-out:

Role #1: Focus	**Outside-in:** Change leaders set the direction and pace of the organization, identify the critical goals, and set the strategic priorities of the change to achieve the desired results. **Inside-out:** Leaders first become committed to the change themselves, then champion the change through effective, focused communication. They work hard to get everyone to understand what, why, when, and how the change will happen. They apply change principles consistently at all three levels of the organization—individual, team, and organization.

Role #2:
Align

Outside-in: Change leaders align stakeholder needs, business outcomes, and the processes, structure, and systems of the organization to achieve the new desired results. American writer Upton Sinclair said, "It is difficult to get a man to understand something when his salary depends upon his not understanding it." Leaders work to remove these types of system barriers to open the way for individual alignment.

Inside-out: Change leaders define the needed behaviors that lead to desired results, then ensure the organizational architecture fosters rather than inhibits behavior change. They align people to the technical changes by fostering and rewarding the desired behaviors.

Role #3:
Engage

Outside-in: Extrinsic motivators help drive engagement, and leaders play a vital role in fostering conditions that boost engagement, such as creating an effective culture, enabling leadership development, aligning reward and recognition systems, and empowering decision making at the appropriate levels.

Inside-out: Effective leaders of change also know that individuals own their own behaviors of engagement. Leaders enable commitment to the new vision, values, and strategic direction. Leaders enable employees to give up what they have now for something they want in the future. And this requires changing what they do that is comfortable for something that might not be that comfortable in the short term. Mark Twain said, "Habit is habit, and not to be flung out of the window by any man, but coaxed downstairs a step at a time." Leaders who engage employees' heads, hands, and hearts can implement almost anything.

| Role #4: Lead | **Outside-in:** Change leaders inspire personal and team leadership in others. American author Maya Angelou said, "A leader sees greatness in other people. You can't be much of a leader if all you see is yourself."[12] Great change leaders provide opportunities for their people to stretch and grow. They establish change champions within the organization as a way to develop individual leadership skills and infuse the culture with support for the change.

Inside-out: Great change leaders first transform themselves. Leadership experts Bob Anderson and Bill Adams have found that "when [leaders] try to change the system, [they] run smack into themselves. The organization will never perform at a higher level than the consciousness of its leadership. We only see transformations succeed when senior leaders choose to 'do their work' of mastering leadership and then go on to sponsor and support the entire leadership system in doing this same deep work."[13] |
| --- | --- |
| Role #5: Sustain | **Outside-in:** Too often the great work of change teams gets thrown over the wall to the business to implement, which results in the initiative being only partially successful. But ownership has to be agreed to and accepted, which usually requires more than a mere handoff. The secret to sustainability is that leaders hand off each change project one at a time and ensure that it becomes owned by the business. Effective change leaders work to manage the implementation, clear roadblocks, and ensure that stakeholders aren't confused about priorities.

Inside-out: Institutionalizing change is perhaps one of the most difficult leadership challenges that executives encounter in their professional life. Jack Welch said, "There is no edict in the world that will make people take risks." For some individuals, change is risky. The role of the change leader is to engage employees in the implementation so that they own the changes and can integrate the new, required behaviors into how they do their work. |

Author and organizational consultant Warren Bennis said, "A lack of self-knowledge is the most common, every-day source of leadership failures." Being an effective change leader requires self-awareness of one's own effectiveness in all five roles—Focus, Align, Engage, Lead, and Sustain. It doesn't matter if you are a senior leader over thousands or a project leader with no direct reports. It doesn't matter if you are receiving change or leading change. The patterns for effective change are the same. Leadership is not a position; it's a role. And our experience has shown that leaders who play all five roles successfully transform their own performance as well as the results of their organizations.

Just a note about leadership. After leading change efforts for many years, we know that almost anyone can get really good at the change process. In this book, we are even going to tell you how. We will tell you what works and what to avoid. We will give you models and templates. And we will help you approach change in a way that engages stakeholders. But unless we also help leaders change, the change process will stall and business performance will suffer. To accelerate change, we must accelerate leadership! The leadership lessons learned by experience and the school of hard knocks take too long and will not prepare leaders to respond quickly enough to the new complexities of their business environment. The consequence of falling behind the pace of change will result in competitive disadvantage, or worse—irrelevance and extinction.

In short, leadership matters! And if leaders are going to improve the performance of their business by initiating change, they must also improve the capacity and capability of leadership. Not only must leaders get better at the process of change, they must also transform their individual leadership as well as the collective leadership effectiveness in the organization in order to improve fundamental performance. Increasing individual leadership capacity and evolving leadership team effectiveness are rarely the focus of most transformation efforts; as a result, performance improvement becomes unsustainable. It's not surprising that 70% of change initiatives fail to achieve desired results.

To truly transform an organization and create lasting change, leaders must improve the performance of the business (the process of change), and increase the effectiveness of leadership (the leadership of change). Consequently, the rest of this book is organized around the five roles of great change leaders. When done well, these roles will enable leaders to transform their business, improve results, and build an engaged culture—in short, better organizational efficiency and effectiveness.

SUMMARY

If we revisit the quote from the beginning of the chapter, it would be easy to label Machiavelli as a change pessimist. Phrases like "nothing more difficult," "more doubtful of success," and "more dangerous" could easily discourage the most courageous of heart. Why would anybody embark on such an adventure, no matter how bright the vision of change may be? Yet careful analysis of the Italian politician's insights could also yield a less pessimistic and a more realistic view of change. Yes, it's hard; there are enemies to change; and it's going to take effort to overcome the "lukewarmness" of the status quo. But the real secret to change comes from doing the hard things, not just the easy, fast, or short-term things.

By approaching change from the outside-in *and* the inside-out, change leaders can overcome organizational obstacles and enable individual behavior. As leaders play their roles well, "incredulity" will be overcome by belief. And as leaders proactively pull all the elements of change together to create sustainability at every level of the organization, even the most die-hard "defenders" of the status quo will want to be a part of the "new order of things."

In the chapters that follow, we'll show you how to manage and blend the five roles of great change leaders to create and shape the future state of your organization. When these roles are played well, it changes how leaders at every level (1) think and talk about change, (2) approach change, and (3) elevate what they do as a leader of change.

2

ACCELERATING FOCUS

"You can tell whether a man is clever by his answers.
You can tell whether a man is wise by his questions."

—Naguib Mahfouz, Egyptian writer and winner of
the 1988 Nobel Prize for Literature

The story about Andy Grove and Gordon Moore at Intel getting out of the memory chip business has been retold so often that many of our clients believe it's more legend than fact. But the lessons the story teaches are so important to change they are worth retelling.

In 1985, Andy Grove was the president of Intel and Gordon Moore was the chairman and CEO. The company's core business—its very heart, soul, and identity—was memory chips. They were sitting in Grove's office at Intel. At the time, the company was caught in a price war with the Japanese. Grove described this critical moment in Intel's history this way:

I looked out the window at the Ferris wheel of the Great America amusement park revolving in the distance, then I turned back to Gordon and I asked, "If we got kicked out and the Board brought in a new CEO, what do you think he would do?" Gordon answered without hesitation, "He would get us out of memories." I stared at him, numb, then said, "Why shouldn't you and I walk out the door, come back, and do it ourselves?"[1]

It was a pivotal moment—one that altered the direction of Intel for the better. It was a decision that took courage and leadership. It's an example that has caused countless debates in graduate schools around the globe as future leaders try to anticipate what they would have done if they had been running the show.

When you initiate change, whether you are the head of a well-known Fortune 500 organization or running a small team in charge of quality for your organization's most important product, you are defining a critical inflection point that must be maneuvered effectively. The key change leadership skill required at the inflection point—the point of change—is your ability to *accelerate focus*.

An African native walking through Manhattan said, "They don't see the sky." Your job as a leader is to help people focus on the change amidst the turmoil of the everyday business that is going on around them. They need to clearly see what is critical, why they need to make the change now, why it's important to them, and in some cases, why they should leave behind old behaviors, processes, and ingrained cultural norms to venture into the unknown "new land" with you. Such inflection points cause confusion for people and can become frustrating for leaders when results aren't achieved fast enough. While the newness of the strategic shift can be exhilarating, the difficulty of the execution can be exhausting. When employees can't break with old ways that are no longer helping the organization's performance, the opportunity to catapult to a higher level of achievement is squandered. Accelerating focus clarifies for people why the organization is changing, what they should be doing, what the benefit will be, and how the team will get there.

...

"If existing management wants to keep their jobs when the basics of the business are undergoing profound change, they must adopt an outsider's intellectual objectivity."

—Andy Grove, former chairman and CEO, Intel Corporation

When we were hired to help one of our clients lead a large change effort, we began by interviewing the top fifteen to twenty senior leaders to talk about what was working in the organization and what wasn't. A consistent theme emerged from these interviews—people didn't understand the direction of the organization. Somewhat surprised (given that we were talking to the most senior leaders who should have understood the direction of the firm), we asked, "What is the vision of the organization?" To which we heard the answer numerous times, "We're going to Oregon."

Not sure exactly what that meant, we brought it up with the CEO during our assessment summary. He became angry and said, "These people just don't get it! They want to know all the details of the plan, like when we are going to cross each of the rivers." Becoming even more confused, we asked what people meant when they said, "We're going to Oregon." The CEO explained that it was merely a metaphor he was using to describe how the company needed to fundamentally change everything about how it did business. His desired message was that the process of change would be like traveling to a new land and having to make their own way. Not a bad analogy, but that's not how the message was received by other leaders and employees. In fact, people didn't even understand it was a metaphor at all. They thought the CEO was literally relocating the firm from the Southeast to the Northwest. Imagine the anxiety and uncertainty the CEO unintentionally created with his people by being unclear about his vision for change.

...

"Our plans miscarry because they have no aim. When a man does not know what harbor he is making for, no wind is the right wind."

—Seneca the Younger, Roman statesman

If this example seems a bit comical and far fetched, statistics prove that it happens more often than you'd imagine in many organizations trying to reinvent their business. A study by BlessingWhite found that "If senior leaders aren't crystal clear—and in complete agreement—about the organization's priorities, attempts to cascade their message will be like a crack in a foundation, with the fissure growing larger and larger as communications work their way through the organization."[2] In other words, a metaphor about "going to Oregon" can quickly become a literal "going to Oregon" as communication spreads out and down within a company.

Research shows the widespread lack of focus:

- 95% of workers don't understand their organization's strategy.[3]

- Only 15% of employees can identify one of the top three goals of the company.[4]

- Even those who know the goal lack the commitment to achieve it. Only 51% reported being passionate about the team's goal.[5]

- 81% of employees said they are not held accountable for regular progress on organizational goals.[6]

- And 87% of employees had no clear idea what they should be doing to achieve the goal.[7]

Our experience is that strategic alignment statistics parallel change alignment statistics. If only 15–20% of leaders and employees know their organization's strategic priorities, and spend only 50% of their time accomplishing those priorities, then you'll see the same percentages when you try to introduce a new order of things.

When people in organizations don't understand why things are changing or don't get the vision for the future, it's very hard for them to align their behavior accordingly. The result is that change never happens—teams and organizations miss the critical inflection point and remain in the status quo until they are pushed out of the marketplace. Unless leaders share a unified view of the change and can effectively transmit that view to the people who will implement the change, then people, processes, and systems won't align to deliver the strategic priorities.

...

"History marches to the drum of a clear idea."

—W. H. Auden, Anglo-American poet

WHAT YOU SEE IS WHAT YOU GET

In an important study about employee engagement, BlessingWhite discovered that engaged employees are not just committed, passionate, or proud. They also have a clear line of sight on their own future and on the organization's mission and goals. On the other hand, employees who gave the lowest level of contribution and who weren't engaged said they needed "greater clarity about what the organization needs [them] to do and why."[8] This study illustrates why a combined outside-in and inside-out approach to change is so important. The external, competitive marketplace will often dictate a new outside-in view of what needs to change. But until leaders translate that so employees understand it, accept it, and commit to changing their current view, the inside-out behavior change will stall, and new and better results will be sacrificed.

...

**"It isn't that they can't see the solution. It is that
they can't see the problem."**

—G. K. Chesterton, English writer, lay theologian, poet, philosopher

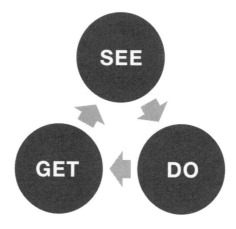

But what comes first—aligning behaviors, changing processes, or clarifying how people see the future? Franklin Covey's See-Do-Get cycle[9] is one of the simplest (yet most impactful) change methods that helps accelerate focus. Instead of beginning with behavior—what you want people to *do* differently, leaders begin with focus—how they want people to *see* the problem and the need for change. If leaders want to get different results through different behavior, they must first help other leaders and employees see things differently. In a change effort, this means everyone must have a clear, common focus on why things are changing, the priorities of the change, and what people need to do differently because of the change.

...

"We must look at the lens through which we see the world, as well as the world we see. The lens itself shapes how we interpret the world."

—Stephen R. Covey, author of *The 7 Habits of Highly Effective People*

When Tony was a young father, like most dads he wanted to develop a great relationship with his children. Part of his process was to play with them. With his son, Timothy, they both loved to play sports. They would often be in the yard throwing a football or baseball whenever the opportunity arose, pretending to be part of the final play in the last seconds of the Super Bowl or World Series. His daughter, Morgan, loved to play board games. One game she loved to play was tic-tac-toe. At seven years old, she was quite good. She learned how to beat Tony every time. One day, Tony was putting some clean clothes in Morgan's closet and found a score sheet on the back of her door titled "Dad/Morgan tic-tac-toe competition." The score read "Morgan 27 wins, Dad 1 win." Tony was amazed at Morgan's competitive spirit.

How does this relate to accelerating focus in change? In a recent executive course, we taught change to a Fortune 50 client, and we played a grown-up game of tic-tac-toe (which we call Tic-Tac-Tony). In this game, each player draws a ten-by-ten grid on a piece of paper. Players pair up and choose who will be the X and who will be the O. We instruct the leaders to get as many points as they can in two minutes. (A point is scored by getting four Xs or Os in a row; and players can add an X or an O to a set of four already played and score again.)

The results are fascinating whenever we play this game with leaders. More often than not, executives compete with each other by blocking and attacking their opponent on the game board. With this particular client, we stopped the game after two minutes and asked participants to tally their scores. Not surprisingly, the results were low with scores of 1-1, 2-1, and 1-0. Real competitive battles. But one team had a very different score: 47. Everyone in the session was amazed (and a bit perplexed). How could this happen?

As we looked into the results, we found that the majority of the teams approached the exercise as a competition. The result? Low scores. For the players who saw the game as a win-lose situation, they actively worked *against* their partner to block each other's progress. But the outlier team that scored 47 saw this activity as a win-win situation. They played to get as many points as they could together as a team. Instead of competing, they cooperated—hence their high score. The message was clear—how you *see* the game influences what you *do* and the result you *get*.

Not surprisingly, the dynamics of the Tic-Tac-Tony game play out identically during organizational change. Over and over again, we see leaders who want different results—a worthy goal, in most cases. And they hope the things they say and try to institutionalize will produce a change in behavior. In other words, they hope for a different result by working on what people *do*. In reality, the greatest leverage and opportunity for success in change is to work on how people *see* the situation—their focus. And that requires leadership!

In Tic-Tac-Tony, players who have a paradigm of cooperation play differently than those who want to compete and win. In a change process, communicating with people about the business case for change, involving them in the problem, getting them engaged in the solution, and working as a team helps them *see* the situation differently and come up with better, more sustainable solutions. In short, what people believe will, in fact, influence their actions and produce different results.

The questions Andy Grove asked were critical: "If we got kicked out and the board brought in a new CEO, what do you think he would do? [So] why shouldn't you and I walk out the door, come back, and do it ourselves?" These questions forced a new way to look at the problem, which led to new behaviors and different results. History is full of examples (Nelson Mandela, Mahatma Gandhi, George Washington) of people who changed their situation by changing their view of the world. Like going to the eye doctor to check your vision, a leader of change must constantly ask, "Which is clearer, A or B, C or D?" When the vision for change gets clearer and clearer, transformations accelerate as more and more people see the landscape of the future the same and start working toward a common goal.

...

"The best way to predict the future is to create it."

—Peter Drucker, Austrian-born American
management consultant, educator, and author

DO YOU HAVE FOCUS?

How do you know if your organization has a common focus for the change you're trying to implement, or if you fall in line with those organizations mentioned earlier where only 15% of employees can identify the top goals and priorities of the company? You have a couple of options that will help determine if your change is focused.

First, you could conduct a survey to find out if people are seeing the change correctly and uniformly. Survey results will tell you the exact percentages about employees' level of understanding, engagement, and allocation of time. A survey is well worth the investment in time and resources to measure focus. It provides you with analytical data that you can do something about.

Second, some of our clients have used what we call a 5 x 5 x 5 process to assess clarity of the focus. The idea is simple and not as costly as a survey—ask five questions of five leaders and five employees. Of course you can go broader and deeper in the organization, but the 5 x 5 x 5 will get you started and give you a pulse on what people know and will do in your change initiative. Part of your job as a leader of change is to act like an investigative reporter and find out as much as possible in a short amount of time. The five questions you should ask are similar to a reporter's questions:

- What is changing in the organization?

- Why is it changing at this time? What happens if we don't change?

- How will we change? How will we remain the same? How and why do we need to be different?

- Who will be involved?

- When will this take place?

When you pose these questions to other peers and leaders in the organization, you can determine from the responses if people are aligned with the same vision for the change. Do people have the same focus and use the same language? Do people have the same focus, but use different words to describe it? Do people have vastly different focuses, but use the same words to describe it (think "Going to Oregon")? Do people see things differently, describe things differently, and have a different vision for the future? Have they internalized the focus and aligned their actions accordingly? When leaders pose these questions to a smattering of employees across the organization, it becomes clear how well people understand (from the outside-in) and align their behaviors to the focus of the change (from the inside-out). Only then can leaders creatively solve business challenges at all levels.

Indra Nooyi, CEO of PepsiCo, commented on her turnaround of the company during a year of Wall Street murmurings about its potential breakup: "It takes great courage to live in the moment and look beyond it at the same time."[10] An often-used metaphor that echoes Nooyi's words is that change is like heading the car in a new direction while trying to change the tires. Taking it one step further, you could also say that many changes have the extra challenges of having multiple drivers wanting to go in different directions while others are arguing about which tires to change, how to change them, and when. Obviously, the car is going to crash. It takes great courage for a leader of change to define the new destination of an organization; it takes even greater courage and stamina to get everyone on board and see it through to the end.

...

"Tactics is knowing what to do when there is something to do; strategy is knowing what to do when there is nothing to do."
—Savielly Tartakower, leading Polish and French chess grandmaster

We see problems with focus manifested in two ways: (1) leaders don't have a defined, easily recognizable vision for the change; and (2) leaders don't translate that vision so employees understand and care. Archimedes, an ancient Greek mathematician, said, "Give me a lever long enough and a fulcrum on which to place it, and I shall move the world." While there are many tools available to overcome these two focus problems, we have found great success with our clients using the following five. In the pages that follow, we will provide an overview for each one (with a little more detail on change measures and change strategy, due to their criticality and how few times we have seen them done effectively).

- Business Case for Change

- Change Charter

- FROM → TO Behavior Descriptions

- Change Measures

- Change Strategy

...

**"Man is so made that when anything fires his soul,
impossibilities vanish."**

—Jean De La Fontaine, French poet of the seventeenth century

BUSINESS CASE FOR CHANGE

A common problem in large-scale change efforts is for middle management and change agents to spend an enormous amount of time and energy trying to determine exactly what senior leaders want and how committed they are to change. Too often priorities are unclear. We hear managers say, "It seems like everything is a priority, and we are not doing any of them well." If left unchecked, two common barriers emerge that can derail change implementation:

- **Loss of focus and momentum:** Leadership and management can be distracted from the change by the daily demands of the business. As perceived priorities shift and leaders' time and attention go elsewhere, the change project can lose momentum and focus.

- **Resistance to change:** Change will always be met with resistance. Some resistance is open and obvious; much of it is quiet passivity. Either way, if not managed, resistance to change in any form can drain the energy from a change initiative.

How then can leaders and change agents maintain energy and focus during change? One way is by creating a clear and dynamic case for change that establishes a strong sense of urgency and generates enthusiasm and willingness to change among employees. As leaders communicate with stakeholders throughout the business, they can leverage the case for change repeatedly to sustain momentum and focus. A well-leveraged business case for change can remind everyone why the change was started in the first place.

An effective business case for change includes the following elements:[11]

- **Describes why the current situation is unacceptable in a clear and meaningful way:** includes historical information, internal statistics, and marketplace data

- **Describes the projected cost of not changing:** defines the business risks and costs qualitatively and quantitatively

- **Paints a compelling picture of the desired future state:** includes the benefits of change and concrete, quantitative, and qualitative goals

- **Provides a general strategic path to attain the desired future state:** informs employees of the general path the change will take

- **Produces a felt need for change within employees:** creates a "burning platform" that compels people to accept change

Creating the case for change provides an important opportunity for leaders to include others in the change process. Employees often have compelling data that management might not have that can increase the leverage and effectiveness of the case for change. And it effectively combines the outside-in direction of leaders with the inside-out perspective of employees.

A case for change can take many forms. Some are written as memos, presentations, or a series of questions and answers; others are more visual. The key is to leverage the business case for change in all communication and presentations. We first learned about the power of a good business case for change while working with a cable manufacturer in the Midwest. The organization was trying to implement a change, but they couldn't get any traction with employees on the shop floor because they knew they were the number one volume-producing site in the company. So why bother changing? We sent memos, we had "all hands" meetings, and we talked one-on-one with workers. No change. It wasn't until we created a chart that showed bonuses under the old measurement system versus bonuses under the new measures that we got their attention. What workers had failed to understand (and what we had failed to communicate) was that the organization was going to base bonuses not just on volume and throughput, as it had in the past, but also on scrap rate. That fact didn't become real for employees until they saw it in their take-home pay.

Following is a list of questions that your business case for change should answer to create focus and compelling reasons for change.

Business Case for Change Questions

- What has been the business performance for the past 6–12 months?
- How productive and profitable is the organization compared to competitors?
- What is changing in the industry that warrants a change now?
- What (if any) are the threats to the business?
- What are the critical needs of the business that are not being met?
- What are the concerns of current customers and other key stakeholders?
- What are the current performance gaps, shortfalls, or challenges the organization is experiencing?
- What is the cost of not changing?
- What improvement efforts has the organization used in the past, and how successfully were they implemented? What will be different this time?
- What are the most important reasons and benefits to change?

CHANGE CHARTER

A change charter is a summary of the vision and answers important questions about the change. The purpose of chartering the change work is to craft the right message so it can be communicated regularly and consistently. When the charter is clear and engaging, leaders and employees understand the "why" behind the change and start engaging in the "how."

A potential client sent us a sixteen-page charter document to help us understand the change they were beginning and to determine how we might add value. They asked us, "What do you think of the charter?" likely hoping for a positive response from us. We didn't like it at all. Charters are summaries, not tomes. If you can't explain what your change initiative is about in one page (maybe two), you aren't clear about it yourself. A good charter briefly answers key questions for employees and leaders, such as these:

- What is changing and why?

- Why should I care?

- What do I need to be aware of?

- What will be the implications for my job?

- How big of a deal is this?

- How hard will it be?

- How much energy will be required?

...

"He who has a *why* can endure any *how*."

—Friedrich Nietzsche, German philosopher, cultural critic, poet, composer, and Latin and Greek scholar

The following charter elements can be used in casual conversation or formal presentations, or they can be summarized in a communication template and distributed throughout the business.

Charter Elements

Problem Statement (Current State)

- What pain are we or our stakeholders experiencing?
- What is wrong or not working?
- What is the value proposition of the change?

Goal Statement (Desired State)

- What gain are we hoping to realize?
- What needs to change to get us there?
- If the gain is fully realized, what will be the outcome?
- How should people behave differently?

Business Impact

- Why should we do this?
- What will be the business impact? What will be the people impact?
- How does this change project align with the business strategy?
- What is the priority of the project? How does this compare in priority to other major projects in the business right now?

Project Scope

- What are the boundaries of the initiative? What's in? What's out?
- What authority do we have?
- How does this need to integrate with other projects or initiatives?

Measures

- What are the major milestones?
- How will we know if we are successful?
- How will we measure engagement, utilization, and adoption?

Change Team

- Who are the change team members?
- What are their roles?
- How much of their time will be dedicated to the project?

FROM → TO BEHAVIOR DESCRIPTIONS

During another client engagement with a leading utility in the United States, we were facilitating a critical working session with a senior leadership team regarding a large-scale change effort. The business was facing a major downturn (if not extinction) if things did not change in a hurry. The CEO was in the front of the room with us. We were describing the changes to the strategy, systems, and processes in a seemingly elegant manner. Thinking that everyone listening was highly engaged and on the same page, we were about to move on to the next critical area when Randy, the Chief Technical Officer, raised his hand. He was one of the smartest and most quietly confident people on the team. We will never forget his question, which he asked without any anger or challenge. "I get all of the rationale, the vision, the strategy, and even the process issues, but what I don't get is what you want me to do differently."

Our presentation came to an abrupt stop. We recoiled in disbelief from his question. How could he not know? Surely a senior executive should know that answer. As we explored further, it became clear that he wasn't the only person in the room uncertain about what to do differently. Randy's question became a defining moment in the change effort.

Randy's question uncovered an often unattended shortcoming in focusing change efforts—clarifying the changes in behavior that need to happen. As a result of that experience, we have built great discipline, planning, focus, and engagement around identifying what we call FROM → TO behaviors. For many employees, organizational change can feel complex and difficult. But at its most basic level, change is first about focus (see) and then about behavior (do). Part of establishing a compelling focus is to clearly define the behaviors you want people to stop and to start doing in service of the new goals or desired culture. What Randy was really asking was, "What should I *stop* doing, *start* doing, and *continue* doing? How should I change how I spend my time? Do I need to learn new skills? Are there new tools, new focus points, new stakeholders, and new results that I need to put in my plan of how I execute day-to-day?" The answers to these questions are the FROM → TO behavior descriptions that add to your focus.

Here are some FROM → TO descriptions our client articulated at a high level in response to Randy's question:

- FROM operational efficiency focus TO operational excellence focus

- FROM responding to customers TO proactively serving customers

- FROM a culture of "can do" TO a culture of "must do"

- FROM leaders holding employees accountable TO everyone being accountable

- FROM individual work focus TO a team approach and team rewards

- FROM caring about the customer TO proving customer care by attaining the #1 nationally rated ACSI customer service

- FROM leaders fighting fires TO leaders allocating time in their calendars to focus on strategic issues

The impact of defining the FROM → TO behaviors for this utility was monumental. It enabled the transformation, survival, and ultimate success of the company. Being able to share not only what was changing and why, but what exactly people should be doing differently solidified the focus for Randy and for everyone else. Each person could confidently say, "This is *why* we're changing; this is *how* we're changing; and this is *what* I need to do differently."

CHANGE MEASURES

Changing business results is about changing behavior, and changing behavior is greatly enabled by measurement. Business management author Tom Peters said, "What gets measured gets done." To truly understand the importance of measurement in change, you have to look deeply into the anatomy of a change effort. Peter Drucker often said that all grand strategies must eventually degenerate into work. Said another way, organizations don't change, people do. Until the focus is translated into what people do, change won't happen. Consequently, to measure change you must understand the fundamental things that are changing—at the work level. Once people understand the FROM → TO behaviors expected of them (described in the previous section), then leaders can build measures to gauge the new behaviors and the results.

...

"What is important is seldom urgent,

and what is urgent is seldom important."

—Dwight D. Eisenhower, former US president

Let us share a sports example to illustrate. We both enjoy basketball and played competitively when we were younger. On a trip to New York City, Tony was walking around lower Manhattan and came across an outdoor basketball court. He stopped to watch a large group of local young men playing a pick-up game. The game was very competitive and spirited. Even from afar, it was easy to tell that the players were keeping score just by the level of intensity and focus. Two other teams were waiting to take on the winner. What were the measures driving the spirited competition? The score! And what was the reward? In addition to "bragging rights," the winning team got to stay on the court and continue playing, while the losing players had to sit and watch until they got a chance to play again.

How was this game different from any other pick-up game on a local playground? The players were keeping score and had defined rewards for winning. Because they were keeping score, they were playing hard, intense basketball. People play differently when they are keeping score—when they are being measured in some way. If players are just shooting around or playing for fun, the intensity drops.

The same holds true during times of change. We have learned that effective score-keeping must be very personal, easily observable, and regularly measured and communicated. In other words, if a team is focused on a particular FROM → TO set of behaviors, it's more likely people will change. And if the ABCs of change are included, change is accelerated. We call this the ABC theory of behavior change.

A = Antecedents

B = Behaviors

C = Consequences

The antecedents (A) are the actions taken to set the change process in motion, things such as communicating goals, providing training, setting sales incentives, establishing new processes, and implementing new rewards, just to name a few. Typically, leaders spend a great deal of time planning and organizing antecedents (A) to set up the change for success. Antecedents (A) are necessary, but not sufficient for transformation to occur.

The B in the ABCs of change is key. The B represents the FROM → TO behaviors that will transform the results from good to great. As we mentioned previously, it's vital to get clear and granular about the behaviors (B). All of the antecedents (A) should in some way encourage the new behaviors (B). And all of the new behaviors (B) should be regularly measured and have specific consequences (C) attached.

The C represents the consequences, both positive and negative, for the defined behaviors (B). Positive consequences (C) can be rewards, money, time off, praise, recognition, promotions, etc. Negative consequences can be discipline, demotions, reduced bonuses, etc. For a consequence to accelerate behavior change, make sure that (1) the consequence is a natural result of the behavior, (2) it is reported close to the event, and (3) it is within the person's control.

The most interesting thing about the ABC formula is that the consequences (C) carry four times the value of the antecedents (A) in creating behavior (B) change. What this means is that leaders can do a great job setting up the change, but if they don't hold people accountable, the change will likely fail. We all know this intuitively, and yet we often don't follow up with rigorous measurements and consequences. Instead, we move on to the next "shiny object" (as one of our clients used to say) hoping it will create the change we need.

A good example that illustrates the ABC formula is how often doctors wash their hands in hospitals. One hospital conducted a study to determine if doctors were washing their hands in between each patient to prevent the spread of germs. The doctors self-reported washing their hands between seeing patients 73% of the time. But the nurses, who were also asked to rate the doctors based on what they observed, reported that doctors washed their hands only 9% of the time.

Another hospital, Cedars-Sinai in Los Angeles, California, did a similar study and discovered its doctors washed their hands between visiting patients 65% of the time. While that was certainly better than 9%, it still meant that 35% of the time doctors were not disinfecting their hands before treating patients. The hospital administration was in disbelief. Their doctors, the people who knew the most about how germs and disease spread, simply were not in the habit of washing their hands. How could they change that?

The hospital tried everything to get the doctors to improve, including education programs, reminders, banners with catchy slogans, emails, and Starbucks gift cards to those with the best hand-washing records. Many of these activities could be considered the antecedents (A) administrators took to change behavior. But none of these programs were successful because they failed to package ABC together in a meaningful way for the doctors.

Then Cedars-Sinai administrators decided to clearly link A, B, and C. The antecedents (A) were the educational programs and reminders. The behavior (B) was FROM washing their hands occasionally between patients TO washing their hands every time between patients. Finally, they implemented two powerful consequences (C). In this case, they chose negative consequences. First, they took hand samples from doctors and grew them in petri dishes for a few weeks. Then they took pictures of what had grown in the petri dishes and turned them into computer screen savers. Those disgusting images reminded the doctors of everything they were passing around on their hands when they didn't wash. The second thing administrators did was publicly publish on a weekly basis the names of doctors who failed to wash their hands. Nobody wanted to be on that list! Cedars-Sinai's doctors responded to the change because the ABC formula was tightly connected and implemented. Soon the hand-washing rates at this hospital were close to 100%.[12]

...

**"Your ability to divert your attention from
activities of lower value to activities of higher value
is central to everything you accomplish in life."**

—Brian Tracy, business author and speaker

Learnings? The ABC formula only works when those elements are connected and implemented in a meaningful way for people; in other words, people must know what to do and how to do it, and they need to feel the immediate pain or gain of the consequence. One study found that 65% of business initiatives required significant behavioral

(B) change on the part of frontline employees.[13] How can leaders enable the shift? Use antecedents (A) to help set up the change, and then establish mechanisms to hold people accountable with consequences (C) to help them pay attention and act differently.

Changes are most impactful when the consequences are so tightly connected to the behavior they reinforce that they motivate the desired change.

Measurement that Enables Real Change

After working with leaders and teams in all kinds of industries and government agencies worldwide, we have learned that in addition to deciding what behaviors need to change, great leaders determine how to keep score in ways that motivate employees to work their hardest. While change measurement systems are vitally important, they are also difficult to get right. General Bill Creech, fighter pilot and four-star general known as "The Father of the Thunderbirds," described the challenge of measurement in this way:

> Managers don't give themselves the tools with which to track and view objectively how people are performing below. You need a way to know if the barn's on fire before it's in ashes. And in business, I've found that too many managers are still watching P&Ls or growth curves, which don't necessarily give them good indications of where their systems are breaking down, where productivity is lagging. When the bottom-line numbers finally come in and they are disheartening, managers don't have answers as to why it all happened. And so, again, the instinct is to centralize across the board, to set down regulations, to try to micromanage everything from the top.[14]

The system of measurement that we work to install in our change projects includes four components:

1. **Define Change Focus**: What are the two or three most important business goals, outcomes, or objectives of the change initiative?

2. **Establish Change Measures**: How will the team measure achievement of the goals, outcomes, or objectives?

3. **Track Progress**: How will the team show progress on a simple, compelling scorecard?

4. **Create Accountability**: How and when will the team hold each other accountable for results?

...

"Hope is generally a wrong guide, though it is very good company by the way."

—Charles Montagu, Earl of Halifax, British statesman

1. Define Change Focus

Defining the change focus means you identify the two or three most important business goals, outcomes, or objectives of the change initiative. The focus can be gleaned from the change charter and the FROM → TO behavior descriptions. A simple yet important question to ask is "How many outcomes can we realistically complete?" While you may want to change everything, most organizations are successful at impacting only a few. So the first task is to determine the few critical business results you hope will be impacted by the change initiative. You might focus on things like reducing costs, improving the effectiveness of operations, or complying with industry regulations.

If you try to change and measure too much, it will feel like you're focusing on nothing. Consequently, we find too many leaders rushing through project plans and long lists of action steps without a solid sense of the few things that will make all the difference. The critical task, then, is to determine the few most important goals to measure so they will get managed.

2. Establish Change Measures

When it comes to measures, we have found that most leaders rely too heavily on (1) enterprise-wide measures that don't apply to the change specifically; (2) lag measures that give end-of-the-month or quarterly results; and (3) "homespun" measures that are desperate attempts at understanding the impact of change. The most useful measures for leaders of change fall into three categories:

1. Business outcome measures
    - Revenue
    - Profit
    - Costs
    - Injuries
    - Volume
    - Throughput

2. Change impact measures
    - Employee engagement (enabling employees to own the changes and to commit to making change happen)
    - Adoption (how quickly employees adopt the new way of working and new behaviors)
    - Utilization (how many employees are using the new system or process to do their jobs)
    - Proficiency (how skilled employees are at the new process, tool, or system)

3.   Lead and lag measures

   ○ Lag (a historical measure that helps change teams know if they
     hit the target)
   ○ Lead (a predictive measure that helps leaders know they are
     making progress toward the change outcome)

We recommend that leaders and change teams establish measures
in each of these three categories. Business outcome measures are
pretty straightforward, given that most organizations already track
these lag items. Change impact measures aren't tracked as often and
require more work by the change team to determine exactly what
makes sense to measure. It's also critical for change leaders to establish both lead and lag measures for the change. A lag measure tells
you if you've achieved the goal. While lag indicators are important for
company performance, they are typically too far removed from the
behavior change to help people make a connection between how they
must change and how they will be measured. A lead measure tells you
if you are *likely* to achieve the goal. Team members can't change a lag
measure, but a lead measure is usually within their control.

For example, you can't control if you contract a long-term sickness
(a lag measure). But you can control how often you get a good night's
sleep, eat right, exercise, and get a physical exam (all lead measures).
The more you act on the lead measures, the more likely you'll avoid
the lag measure (long-term illness).

One of our clients worked to reduce the amount of traffic on the
only road between town and their main plant. During winter months,
dangerous road conditions and inclement weather regularly caused
accidents and delayed shift changes (lag measures). The change initiative focused on reducing the number of company-sponsored vehicles
and increasing the number of employees riding the bus. An adoption
measure tracked total reduction of company trucks in the motor fleet.
For a time, another lead measure tracked how many leaders turned in

their vehicles voluntarily. A utilization lead measure monitored the number of target stakeholders using the company bus system. All of these measures were easy to check and contributed to lighter traffic on the roads, which resulted in fewer accidents and fewer shift delays.

Chris McChesney, Sean Covey, and Jim Huling, authors of *The 4 Disciplines of Execution*, differentiate the lead and lag measures in this way:

> Lag measures are the tracking measurements of the wildly important goal, and they are usually the ones you spend most of your time praying over. Revenue, profit, market share, and customer satisfaction are all lag measures, meaning that when you receive them, the performance that drove them is already in the past. That's why you're praying—by the time you get a lag measure, you can't fix it. It's history. Lead measures are quite different in that they are the measures of the most high-impact things your team must do to reach the goal. In essence, they measure the new behaviors that will drive success on the lag measures, whether those behaviors are as simple as offering a sample to every customer in the bakery or as complex as adhering to standards in jet-engine design.[15]

...

"The important thing is this: to be able at any moment to sacrifice what we are for what we would become."

—Charles Du Bos, French critic and notable essayist

A personal story might further illustrate the difference between lag and lead measures. Last year, both of us decided to lose ten pounds. To keep things simple, let's assume we wanted to drop from 200 to 190 pounds in three months. Our measure was to individually weigh ourselves weekly and record the results. However, getting on the scale does very little to influence sustainable behavior change. It's a lag indicator of progress. So we focused most of our attention on two lead measures—exercise and caloric intake. We consistently set goals for how much we'd exercise and how much we'd eat, and we tracked our lead measures each day. At the end of each week, we'd step on the scale to see if our lead measures (exercise and caloric intake) were impacting our lag measure (weight). As predicted, the weight started to come off, and we each achieved our goal of losing ten pounds in three months. "Once you've identified your lead measures, they become the key leverage points for achieving your goal."[16] Just as with weight loss, your change initiative lead measures can leverage your ultimate success.

3. Track Progress

Change is truly under way when you start to track your progress. Up to this point, the team has focused on determining the right activities and defining how to keep score. Tracking changes helps everyone know if they are winning or losing and what they can do to influence the score. For many, the excitement of winning can help them balance the pain of change.

When it comes to tracking, the question for change leaders is "How will the team show progress on a simple, compelling scorecard?" Typically the issue isn't tracking the measures themselves; we have clients with reports that seemingly track everything in the business. Instead, the best practice of great change leaders is to track only the essential measures (with an emphasis on the lead measures) that will help their teams clearly see if they are winning or losing.

Following is a scorecard from Kendall's favorite game—baseball. Notice how, in an instant, a viewer can tell what's happening in the game. In this case, the New York Yankees are beating the Toronto

Blue Jays by a score of 2 to 0. Currently, there is a man on second base (shown by the white diamond in the center of the scorecard). It's the bottom of the third inning, noted by the small 3rd with a down arrow in the upper right corner. The pitch count on the batter is 1 ball and 1 strike. There is 1 out in this inning, and the pitcher has already thrown 39 pitches. Baseball is a game of strategy that changes with every pitch. The simple scorecard informs the strategy—how they should play the batter differently based on runners in scoring position, how many outs are needed to end the inning, and how likely the hitter will be to swing at a pitch with a 1-1 count. In other words, the scorecard informs strategy and required behavior.

Other simple scorecards exist in almost all aspects of life—from simple charts that track calories, exercise, and weight, to electronic gauges in your car that let you know gas levels, temperature levels, and tire pressure.

One of our clients, an integrated shipyard repair facility, had a complex operation repairing and maintaining every type of US Navy ship in the fleet, from aircraft carriers to battleships and submarines, and refueling every type of propulsion system, from coal to oil and nuclear. In our initial work with the captain of the shipyard and his team, we discovered hundreds of measures—all important for division leaders to understand how their operations were functioning. But these divisional measures didn't indicate overall health of the shipyard. Because we couldn't reduce the number of measures that needed to be tracked for each area, we created a set of composite measures that focused on the four to five critical indicators we had to keep our eye on for the overall change to be successful.

Another client wanted to reduce the number of eye injuries from three per quarter to zero. If they could meet this goal, it would save the company $300,000 per year. To measure and track progress, they selected the following lead change measures:

- **Speed of Adoption**: Number of shop floor workers who started wearing safety glasses within three months

- **Proficiency**: Employees knowing where and when to wear safety glasses (measured by recorded violations)

- **Utilization**: Percentage of employees wearing safety glasses at the end of three months

They constructed a simple scorecard that helped the team track progress and modify change plans, as needed. At the end of three months, 98% of employees were wearing safety glasses at the appropriate times and places. Eye injuries fell from three per quarter to two per year—not quite the goal, but significant progress.

Leaders of change are like coaches who utilize simple scorecards to establish the goal, track progress, and help team members easily see if they are winning.

4. Create Accountability

The final question for leaders in measuring change is "How and when will the team hold each other accountable for results?" In one study, 46% of the organizations surveyed did not have formal systems to execute their strategy. And of these, 73% reported average to below-average performance of their strategies. However, of the 54% that had a formal execution system, 70% out-performed their peer group.[17]

Successful change efforts have a two-part change measurement system. The first part includes the measures and the scorecard (discussed previously). The second part of the system—the part that's usually overlooked—includes reviewing progress, planning actions to course correct, and regularly holding the change team accountable for results. At FranklinCovey, they describe it this way:

> The cadence of accountability is a rhythm of regular and frequent meetings of any team that owns a wildly important goal. These meetings happen at least weekly and ideally last no more than twenty to thirty minutes. In that brief time, team members hold each other accountable for producing results . . .[18]

Creating a "cadence of accountability" requires teams to determine the following:

- Frequency of the meeting (we recommend weekly)

- Type of meeting (face-to-face or virtual)

- Meeting attendees

- Length of the meeting (short fifteen-minute scorecard meeting or part of the regular change team meeting)

- Consequences (positive and negative) for fulfilling commitments

- Individual commitments for the coming week

One change team we worked with met at the end of every shift during the shift change. Part of the meeting was to transfer knowledge about production and machinery; part of it was to celebrate successes (and banter a bit). Another team met weekly to track and review the number of missions flown, equipment failures, maintenance procedures, and mission readiness.

Unfortunately, and despite our recommendations, we've had a lot of clients who only meet at the end of the month to discuss monthly or quarterly results (lag measures). These clients have a difficult time keeping focus and energy on the change goals because of the long delay between meetings. And the lag measures they review are too far removed from what change teams can do immediately to make a difference. Great change leaders create a system of measurement that focuses on lead measures, is simple to track and understand, and is used to generate action items for individual team members.

...

"Great minds have purposes, others have wishes."

—Washington Irving, American author, essayist,
biographer, historian, and diplomat

CHANGE STRATEGY

Organizational change is often similar to New Year's resolutions. Change teams do lots of work up front to identify the change and generate excitement, but the initiative is soon forgotten in the haze of the day-to-day business. No business would attempt to operate without a basic business strategy, yet in both personal and organizational change, some mistakenly expect that they can enter into a change process without more than a few "resolutions," some e-mails, and perhaps a company-wide meeting or two.

Like a business strategy, a well-thought change strategy helps a team determine how it will accomplish the objectives of the change. Author Richard Rumelt said that a coherent strategy "focuses resources, energy, and attention on some objectives rather than others."[19] Yet look at organizational success rates with business strategy. A Kaplan and Norton study found that only 10% of employees understand their organization's strategy, only 30% of executives have their goals aligned with the strategy, and only 60% of organizations align their processes with the strategy.[20] Dismal numbers! And sadly, our experience with change strategies parallels these findings. Consequently, the success rate of change initiatives is very low. One author summarized it like this:

> When organizations are unable to make new strategies—when people evade the work of choosing among different paths into the future—then you get vague mom-and-apple-pie goals that everyone can agree on. Such goals are direct evidence of leadership's insufficient will or political power to make or enforce hard choices. Put differently, universal buy-in usually signals the absence of choice.[21]

A travel analogy helps to illustrate the importance of a change strategy. Think about a time when you visited a foreign country. What was your experience? If you're anything like us, foreign trips can be challenging if you don't know the geography, food choices, language, laws, and customs. All of these variables can make you feel uneasy about the new experience. What can be helpful in these situations are things like a map, a translator (or dictionary) to help with the language, and a prioritized list of places you want to visit.

A change effort is analogous to foreign travel in many ways. For people going through change, the new work and behaviors can feel foreign and create a lot of anxiety. Employees might feel a bit lost, unengaged, or frustrated about what to do. A change strategy is like a map or a translator that defines the process the organization will go through to achieve the desired change objectives.

...

"The dogmas of the quiet past are inadequate to the stormy present."

—Abraham Lincoln, former US president

We have been involved in a wide gamut of change initiatives—from the simple to the very complex. Any level of change requires a strategy to overcome the dogmas and norms built up in an organization over time. One of our clients, a major financial services firm, found that its sales force did not focus on customer service for its key products, only on sales of the products. Not a big surprise given that sales people are hired to sell and customer service people are responsible for after-sales solutions, right? But our client knew that business retention was key to profitability because its policies did not mature in value for several years. In this case, the change strategy was a simple one—tweak the compensation system to reward sales less and service/retention more. The strategy worked and profitability soared.

Another client, a commercial bank, wanted to create a culture of service that would foster long-term customer loyalty. But changing culture is more complex than changing a compensation system. That strategy required a change in behaviors, process, leadership practices, hiring, training, and communication. It involved a lot of people working collaboratively across many functions. Finally after several years of change, the bank started to see customer loyalty scores improve and revenue rise.

The point is whether your change initiative is large or small, simple or complex, you need a strategy! Few change efforts are successful without one.

Elements of a Change Strategy

The Battle of Trafalgar, described in Rumelt's book *Good Strategy, Bad Strategy*, exemplifies important elements of a change strategy. In 1805, Napoleon wanted to invade England after gaining the advantage in other key surrounding countries. But to gain access to Britain, he had to control the English Channel. The combined fleet of the Spanish and French Armada numbered thirty-three ships, compared with the smaller British navy numbering twenty-seven ships. The tactics of the day were to stay in line and fire broadside at each other until one side was either sunk or withdrew from the battle. But Admiral Lord Nelson strategized with his British ship captains to take a risk. He divided the fleet into two columns and drove at Napoleon's fleet hitting their line perpendicularly and creating a discontinuity in the battle. Lord Nelson risked his lead ships, hoping to capitalize on the heavy swell that day and the less-trained Franco-Spanish gunners. Betting that his more experienced English captains would outmaneuver their opponents, Nelson won the battle by sinking twenty-two ships in the French and Spanish fleet. Rumelt summarizes, "The core of strategy work is always the same: discovering the critical factors in a situation and designing a way of coordinating and focusing actions to deal with those factors."

...

"Strategy without tactics is the slowest route to victory. Tactics without strategy is the noise before defeat."

—Sun Tzu, military general, strategist, and philosopher

A change strategy helps all involved know the critical factors of change and the actions the change team will take to deal with those factors. Questions we have found helpful to determine the most appropriate strategy for change include these:

- How big is the change? Is it incremental in nature, transitional, or transformational?

- How fast do we need to change?

- How complex is the problem?

- Do we need a major culture change to ensure success?

- Will the solution require a lot of planning and coordination?

- When is it critical that the recipients of change get involved in the solution?

- How will solutions be deployed?

- How will we coordinate alignment of teams throughout the project?

Knowing what is working and not working in the current situation and what the challenges are moving forward, a leader of change can determine the most appropriate way—the best strategy—to lead change.

...

"A rock pile ceases to be a rock pile the moment a single man contemplates it, bearing within him the image of a cathedral."

—Antoine de Saint-Exupéry, French novelist

Change Strategy Approaches

Organizations approach change strategy in different ways. Several years ago, we worked with a client after they had hired a large consulting firm to develop a change strategy. Their approach (typical of many big consulting firms) was top-down, highly analytical, and outside-in. Their consultants conducted the analysis and provided insights to senior leadership, then delivered the findings and solution to the organization to implement. This approach has many advantages. It's fast, it gives the firm access to really smart people, networks are leveraged across the industry to discover best practices, and new alternatives are considered that might not have been previously. The approach also has some distinct disadvantages. When other people do the work and simply hand over a solution, employees often lack understanding, acceptance, and commitment. Implementation is often slow and arduous because of the very narrow base of ownership. And internal experience about what has worked and not worked in the past is minimized.

We have also seen organizations use a facilitated approach with outside consultants leading internal teams to develop solutions. Another approach is to train internal people in change leadership so employees can handle initiatives without the aid of outside consultants.

Our experience is that most leaders of change don't make conscious decisions about the approach they will take. We see far too many leaders and teams jump in quickly and then muddle through a change project because they didn't take the time to think through the implications of each approach.

A number of dimensions should be considered when defining an approach to change that combines both an outside-in and inside-out focus. This list isn't all-inclusive, but these five factors will help clarify the change strategy.

- **Transitional versus Transformational**. What is the nature of the change? Is it incremental or transformational?

Transitional: Less complex; typically involves changing only pieces of the business or processes	Transformational: Highly complex; has implications to many aspects of the business such as process, structure, and culture
Implications: Could rely on a select group of experts; implementation is often quicker; typically good for a smaller, more focused project	Implications: Takes more time and effort; requires more resources; requires more integration across the organization; requires more time; has competing demands
Example: Reorganization of a small functional department	Example: Integration of two business units

- **Top-Down versus Bottom-Up.** Would this change benefit from more direction from the top or more participation throughout the business?

Top-Down: Typically a directive from above; solution crafted by leaders; employees receive solution to be implemented	Bottom-Up: Involves multiple stake-holders from across the business (primarily those who will be affected by the change); allows for input and shaping of the solutions
Implications: Faster start-up time, but longer implementation time; might have a more strategic perspective; requires a lot of engagement activities	Implications: Longer start-up time, but shorter implementation time; needs strong integration and facilita-tion skills; must determine the right stakeholders to involve; involvement enables engagement
Example: Software (e.g., SAP) upgrade	Example: Large sustainability initiative

- **Light Plan versus Rigorous Plan.** Is it better to do a little planning up front and refine as you go, or think through all the details of the initiative and create a thorough plan?

Light Plan: Initial plan created in the beginning but refined during implementation	Rigorous Plan: Energy and resources focused at the beginning of the change project for thorough planning, involvement, communication, etc.
Implications: Requires influencing key people and/or creating a more "viral" approach to adoption	Implications: Requires large up-front investment in planning and prepa-ration with a potentially smaller implementation team
Example: Starting a quality group	Example: Process improvement program

- **Straightforward versus Complex Design.** Is the project well defined, or do solutions need to develop as understanding evolves over time?

Straightforward: Easily understood change vision; defined beginning, middle, and end phases; easily defined list of activities and steps	Complex: Complex change vision; requires the list of activities to evolve over time; difficult to predetermine all of the activities, issues, or levers required
Implications: Initial diagnosis and analysis yields well-defined solutions; little or no complex behavior change required	Implications: Ongoing diagnosis and analysis of issues required throughout the change; some unknown desired outcomes or definitions of success at the beginning of the project
Example: Company-wide implementation of Microsoft Office 2010	Example: Transition from a product-focused to an operational-excellence-focused organization

- **Single-Wave versus Multiple-Wave Implementation.** Does the type of change lend itself to a single-wave rollout or multiple-wave (staggered) rollout?

Single Wave: Aspects of the project are so integral they need to be addressed and implemented in a single phase	Multiple Wave: Complexity of the end result requires multiple phases as the most effective way of accomplishing the end objective
Implications: Intensity of the project could require dedicated resources; requires up-front alignment with stakeholders	Implications: Typically requires multiple and simultaneous projects; requires more sophisticated project management and integration; requires stakeholder involvement at key milestones; likely longer projects requiring more sustained commitment
Example: Merger staffing	Example: Full SAP integration

Plotting and Describing Your Change Strategy

If you were going to describe your change to a colleague, what would you say? If someone asked, "What is your approach?" would you have a response? We have had success encouraging leaders of change to plot their change strategy along a series of continuums based on the five factors previously described. Once you plot your change strategy on each continuum, you will better understand your aggregate approach to change. The example below is from one of our clients moving from a decentralized and independent business model to a more centralized and functional business model.

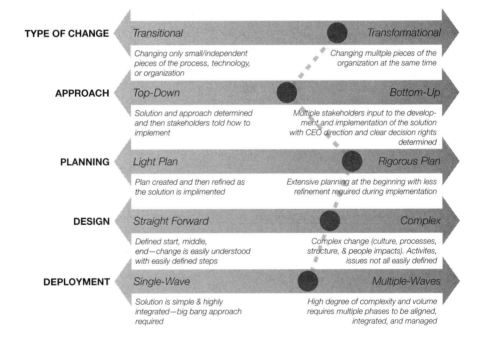

TYPE OF CHANGE	*Transitional*	*Transformational*
	Changing only small/independent pieces of the process, technology, or organization	Changing mulitple pieces of the organization at the same time
APPROACH	*Top-Down*	*Bottom-Up*
	Solution and approach determined and then stakeholders told how to implement	Multiple stakeholders input to the development and implementation of the solution with CEO direction and clear decision rights determined
PLANNING	*Light Plan*	*Rigorous Plan*
	Plan created and then refined as the solution is implimented	Extensive planning at the beginning with less refinement required during implementation
DESIGN	*Straight Forward*	*Complex*
	Defined start, middle, end—change is easily understood with easily defined steps	Complex change (culture, processes, structure, & people impacts). Activites, issues not all easily defined
DEPLOYMENT	*Single-Wave*	*Multiple-Waves*
	Solution is simple & highly integrated—big bang approach required	High degree of complexity and volume requires multiple phases to be aligned, integrated, and managed

After you've defined your strategic approach, we recommend you create a thirty-second "elevator" speech that you can use to describe your change strategy to others. This brief speech helps prepare you for that inevitable question, "How are we going to do this change?"

One format we have used is a simple fill-in-the-blank statement that summarizes each of the five factors. In the case of our client example shown in the previous graphic, a simple summary might have been something like this:

> We have a situation that requires *a transformational approach* to the business (type of change). So our plan will be to engage *multiple stakeholders at all levels in change* (approach). This will require *significant up-front planning* (planning) to deal with the *complex nature of the change* (design). And given the complexity, we will *roll out the change in multiple waves* to the organization (deployment).

Developing a change strategy gives people a way to cogently communicate about the change and align accordingly.

CONCLUSION

Several decades ago, well-known change author John Kotter decreed that organizations and leaders of change have had a dismal record in transformational change efforts. Unfortunately, not much has changed. Too many leaders today still stumble through change haphazardly and add to the "dismal record." People in organizations fail to *see* the problem, the need for change, or the future, so it's hard for them to find new solutions and align their activities accordingly. The result is that change initiatives stumble, stall, or stop completely. Gary Hamel, a best-selling author and American management expert, postulates that change efforts fail because organizations are designed for efficiency and change is disruptive to that end. And yet, despite the disruption, change must happen and happen quickly for organizations to remain solvent.

...

**"Every new truth which has ever been propounded has,
for a time, caused mischief; it has produced discomfort
and oftentimes unhappiness sometimes disturbing social and
religious arrangements, and sometimes merely by the disruption
of old and cherished association of thoughts. . . . And if the truth
is very great as well as very new, the harm is serious."**

—Henry Thomas Buckle, British historian

The first change leadership role required to avoid common blunders is to *accelerate focus.* Accelerating focus clarifies for people what is changing, why the organization is changing, what the expected results will be, and what teams and individuals need to do differently. Using the five tools we covered in this chapter sets a clear and compelling focus—both from the outside-in and from the inside-out:

- Business Case for Change

- Change Charter

- FROM → TO Behavior Descriptions

- Change Measures

- Change Strategy

Whether you are the head of a large organization working on transformational change or running a small team in charge of changing a key process, accelerating the focus of your change will improve the odds of your success. Once your focus is clear, then you are ready to accelerate alignment.

KEY POINTS

- Change leaders need to see themselves as experts in the science of changing people's behavior. In order to do so, they need to be very clear about the behavior that needs to change, the reason for that change, the path to changing that behavior, and the motivation and consequences or support system needed. This is the essence to Change the Way You Change.

- Great change leaders help employees focus on the change amidst the turmoil of the everyday business that is going on around them. Employees need to clearly see what is critical, why they need to make the change now, why it's important to them, and why they should leave behind old behaviors, processes, and ingrained cultural norms to venture into the unknown.

- The external, competitive marketplace will often dictate a new outside-in view of what needs to change. But until leaders translate that so employees understand it, accept it, and commit to changing their current view, the inside-out behavior change will stall, and new and better results will be sacrificed.

- In a change process, communicating with employees about the business case for change, involving them in the problem, getting them engaged in the solution, and working as a team helps them see the situation differently and come up with better, more sustainable solutions.

- An effective business case for change describes why the current situation is unacceptable in a clear and meaningful way, describes the projected cost of not changing, paints a compelling picture of the desired future state, provides a general strategic path to attain the desired future state, and produces a felt need for change within employees.

- A change charter is a summary of the vision and answers important questions about the change. When the charter is clear and engaging, leaders and employees understand the "why" behind the change and start engaging in the "how."

- For many employees, organizational change can feel complex and difficult. But at its most basic level, change is first about focus (see) and then about behavior (do). Part of establishing a compelling focus is to clearly define the behaviors you want people to stop and to start doing in service of the new goals or desired culture.

- Changing business results is about changing behavior, and changing behavior is greatly enabled by measurement. Until the focus is translated into what people do, change won't happen. To measure change you must understand the fundamental things that are changing—at the work level. Good measurement systems have four parts: define change focus, establish change measures, track progress, and create accountability.

- Like a business strategy, a well-thought-out change strategy helps a team determine how it will accomplish the objectives of the change. A change strategy addresses five factors: the nature of the change, the change approach, the amount of up-front planning required, the complexity of the change, and the approach to implementation.

3

ACCELERATING ALIGNMENT

**"Problems cannot be solved with the same
level of thinking that created them."**

—Albert Einstein, theoretical physicist and
developer of the general theory of relativity

S everal years ago, we were asked by the leadership team of a gas refining plant to help improve reliability. The target results were 97% onstream and 88% utilization in two years. The basic idea was to design a process that would help move the organization from a reactive reliability mindset to a proactive one. Initial estimated cost savings per year were about $22 million. These were some of the guidelines given to the team:

- No massive plant-wide structural changes.

- No headcount reductions.

- No changes to contract-negotiated items with the union.

- Solutions had to support the organization's values.

- Solutions had to change the systems, not people.

- Solutions had to have both operator and maintenance involve-ment, engagement, and buy-in.

Not only was the business goal challenging, but the typical "silver bullet" solutions seemed off the table. Going in and just restructuring (a typical approach) wasn't allowed. Laying off people to save money wouldn't be approved. The solutions were going to have to come from somewhere else.

...

"To manage a system effectively, you might focus on the interactions of the parts rather than their behavior taken separately."

—Russell L. Ackoff, organizational theorist

The two groups tasked to improve reliability were the Maintenance and Operations departments. Both groups had significant problems. Maintenance had an inconsistent budget and a scheduling process that would often disrupt operations. Operators would run equipment to the breaking point in an effort to increase shift production. Neither group saw the need to work together. The idea of having operators more involved in the maintenance of the facility was foreign and seemed to violate typical operating procedures.

Early in the project, we brought the two groups together to solve what we thought was an easy problem. We wanted them to gain experience working together and have a "quick win." The two groups assembled and we explained the issue. Pigeons nesting in the pipes of the refinery were creating reliability problems. During the winter months, the pigeons enjoyed nesting in the pipes where leaking steam would keep them warm. But the mess they left behind created problems. What could we do? As operators and maintenance personnel began brainstorming potential solutions, one recommendation was to issue pellet guns to all operators and shoot the pigeons. While the solution was simple and relatively cost effective in the short term, it was not a good idea on many other levels. Animal activists would surely protest, and guns discharging in a gas refinery were a safety issue.

In the book *Influencer*, the authors highlight how tricky it can be to design organizations:

> The problem with sticking to our favorite methods is not that the methods are flawed per se; it's that they're far too simplistic. It's akin to hiking the Himalayas with only a fanny pack. There's nothing wrong with Gatorade and a granola bar, but you'll probably need a lot more. Bringing a simple solution to a complex and resistant problem almost never works.[1]

The pigeon issue was an early finding of the overarching reliability problems. We discovered that the physical factors (pigeons and leaking steam) impacting reliability manifested a deeper issue in the attitude and mindset of Maintenance and Operations. As such, taking care of only the physical issues wouldn't solve the problem. Solutions needed to be holistic and address the cankered mindset, not simply get rid of the birds.

Our experience in the trenches has proven over and over again that great leaders are system thinkers who understand the dynamics and interrelationships between elements of the organization, just as great architects understand the relationship between all the elements that make up a great building.

One group said, "It takes a combination of strategies aimed at a handful of vital behaviors to solve profound and persistent problems."[2] For many years, we have utilized the following simple, yet profound philosophy:

"Organizations are perfectly designed to get the results they get."

Given this philosophy, to accelerate the speed of change and improve performance, leaders must get the right design and alignment of all the processes, structure, and systems in the organization that encourage and enable the correct behaviors and improve results. At a basic level, leaders must become organizational architects (outside-in) able to diagnose what is inhibiting the right behaviors in an organization (inside-out), and then design solutions that are aligned in a way to support long-term, sustainable results.

At the refinery, once the Maintenance personnel and operators understood this principle, the physical solutions for the pigeon problem became clear—wire fencing around critical areas, "dummy" owls to scare the birds away, and repair of steam leaks along critical lines. As time went on, they improved their ability to look at the entire system before determining solutions versus solving only superficial issues. But an even greater benefit emerged in their ability to challenge their mindset—including how they worked together, how they redefined who owned maintenance (expanding the role of operators), and how production schedules and budgets were created and shared.

...

> **"General management is more than stewardship of**
> **individual functions. Its core is strategy: defining and**
> **communicating a company's unique position,**
> **making trade-offs, and forging fit among activities."**
>
> —Michael E. Porter, author and strategist

SOLVE PROBLEMS LIKE GRADUATES FROM KINDERGARTEN

In a classic TED Talk[3] by Tom Wujec (designer of digital tools for teams that create cars, bridges, consumer products, movies, and videogames), he describes a design exercise called the Marshmallow Challenge that was first introduced by Peter Skillman. The challenge is simple: in eighteen minutes, teams of four must build the tallest freestanding structure out of twenty sticks of spaghetti, one yard of tape, one yard of string, and one marshmallow that has to be anchored on top.

After running the simulation more than seventy times, Wujec discovered a few things about top-performing teams. Kindergarteners were consistently among the best-performing groups, and business students were regularly among the worst. The difference is that "business students are trained to create a *single* right plan, then execute on it. When they put a marshmallow on top and the structure topples over, there's no time to fix it, and that creates a crisis!" But according to Wujec, "kindergarteners work differently. They build a little structure, add the marshmallow. They play around and add some more spaghetti sticks. Again and again, they build prototypes each step of the way, always keeping the marshmallow on the top."

It's an ironic finding that those with little education consistently outperform those who have spent time in the sacred halls of academia. But what we think is more interesting (because it supports what we've seen in client organizations) are two other findings from Wujec's running of the simulation. First, "Designers recognize this type of collaboration as the essence of the iterative process—which is central to design thinking." And second, "Design is a contact sport. It demands that we bring all of our senses to the task and apply the very best of our thinking, feeling, and doing to the challenge."

In the case of the gas refinery plant, collaborative teams were able to solve problems that had plagued the plant for years. Bumping into each other's "space" and tackling difficult conversations that had been avoided for a long time helped the teams create systemic solutions. The collaborative process was more than just the creative generation of ideas—it was the discovery of sustainable solutions that were practical for the business and supported by those who had to implement them.

...

"He that will not apply new remedies must expect new evils."

–Francis Bacon, British philosopher

THE MOST OVERLOOKED ACCELERATOR OF CHANGE

In our experience, holistic design is the most overlooked accelerator of change among senior leaders. Why? The list of reasons is long: it's not emphasized in business school programs; it takes time; it can be disruptive to the operation; etc. But the most common reason we've heard is that it's hard. There's no quick-fix solution (like restructuring) that leaders can implement next quarter or use to improve the bottom line by year-end. "Forging fit among activities," as Porter says, requires effort and holistic thinking. Organizational change is like planting a garden. For the garden to be productive, the entire system must be addressed—preparing the soil, planting the seeds, providing nutrients, and allowing time for growth. Like gardeners, business leaders need to look at the entirety of their operations and align all systems to work together to create a high-performance business.

...

"Most managers and leaders put 10% of their energy into selling the problem and 90% into selling the solution to the problem. People aren't in the market for solutions to problems they don't see, acknowledge, and understand."

–William Bridges, author, speaker, and organizational consultant

An expert at this kind of thinking was Sakichi Toyoda. He developed a process called the "5 Whys" within Toyota Motor Corporation during the evolution of its manufacturing methodologies. (The 5 Whys technique was later made popular through *kaizen*, "Lean" manufacturing,

Six Sigma, and Edwards Deming.) This iterative, question-asking technique is designed to understand cause-and-effect relationships and to get to the root of an issue. To illustrate how well it works, think back to an interaction you had with a four-year-old child. Children are the masters at getting to the real issue! For example, you might announce one morning that you are leaving for work. The child asks, "Why?" You respond, "Because I'm expected to be there." The child asks again, "Why?" You may say, "Because we need to make money." To which the child says, "Why?" After four or five whys, you shut down the conversation and go out the door because your four-year-old has discovered that while all of your answers are valid, the core reason why you're going to work is that you're saving for a new boat!

Now apply the 5 Whys technique to your organization. When people start asking "Why?" multiple times, the underlying truth can be revealing, startling, and just plain hard to solve. But that is also where the real problems (and solutions) are unearthed. Multiple studies have shown that 70% of change efforts fail to achieve their desired results. One key reason behind this dismal statistic is that change leaders don't ask the 5 Whys, so their solutions don't address the underlying problems or align the organization to solve those problems. And the consequence is that change efforts fall short of the mark.

...

"The change process [is] a group activity, and unless group norms and behaviors are also transformed, changes to individual behaviors cannot be sustained."

—Paul R. Dannar, change author

WHAT'S IN A NAME?

One day, we received a call from the leader of a change initiative in one of the largest pharmaceutical companies in the world. They were implementing a Lean manufacturing process that would significantly impact two-thirds of their plants. They asked if we "do change." After some inquiry, we discovered that they were six weeks from their "go live" date and were concerned about the understanding, commitment, and buy-in to the change from leaders and employees alike. Sounded like a fun challenge, so we agreed to the work. Knowing that "organizations are perfectly designed to get the results they get" and that they wanted different results (as specified through Lean manufacturing), they would need to address the alignment of the work and support systems (just to name a few).

We tried and tried to help the team identify misalignments that were barriers to Lean and to long-term sustainability. But the idea of alignment didn't resonate with them for some reason. Feeling frustrated (and running out of time), we changed our language from "misalignments" to "risks" associated with the change. The new verbiage caught on, and we were able to help the team discover the many risks of both changing and not changing the new system.

Our learning? Some leaders resonate more with the idea of *alignments* they have to get right for the organization to operate effectively and efficiently. Other leaders resonate more with the idea of *risks* that have to be mitigated to ensure better performance. Regardless of what term is chosen, leaders must work on the systems and structure to remove barriers *and* enable productive behaviors or the change project will fail to fix the business.

Before you panic, please understand that we're not trying to make you process designers or organizational effectiveness experts. Leave that to the professionals! But we know that because this is one of the most overlooked areas in change management, it's something you must have on your radar to ensure great execution. The most basic way to assess alignment is by asking a few simple questions:

- What's aligned in the organization to create the desired behaviors?

- What's at risk if changes to the processes, structure, and systems can't be aligned?

- What's the impact of this change on other groups?

- What collaborations need to happen to enable the adoption of this change?

- What's changing and not changing? What are the implications for the way we do our work?

If all you do with alignment is ask a few good questions, great! You're further ahead than some leaders we have worked with. But if you really want to get it right, you must work at three levels: individual, team, and organizational.

...

"If the entirety of the organization is not aligned with the change effort, the effort will fail."

–Paul R. Dannar, change author

THREE ALIGNMENTS YOU *HAVE TO* GET RIGHT

Great change leaders are organizational architects who diagnose the impediments to change and create remedies for those impediments. Once again, both the inside-out and outside-in approaches are necessary to create alignment. You must focus on aligning individual behavior (inside-out), but also on the functioning of teams and the organization as a whole (outside-in). A critical look at the interrelationship between each of these levels is called systems thinking.

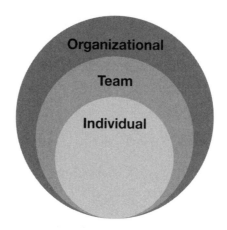

Diagram: Three Levels of Change

Individual Alignment

As we've mentioned before, organizations don't change, people do. Or perhaps said a better way, organizations don't change *until* people do. When leaders inspire individuals to align their behaviors with the new direction of the organization, those individuals will make the difference. We're not suggesting you *change* people. Instead, we're suggesting you help people align their passion and energies with the direction of the change initiative. Thomas Watson, former chairman and CEO of IBM, said, "I believe the real difference between success and failure in an organization can very often be traced to the question of how well the organization brings out the great energies and talents of its people." Instead of changing people, your job is to *engage* them in the change.

So how do you get employees passionate about the change? David Wile, in his book *Why Doers Do*, summarized the many factors that are external and internal to employee engagement, itemized in the following chart.

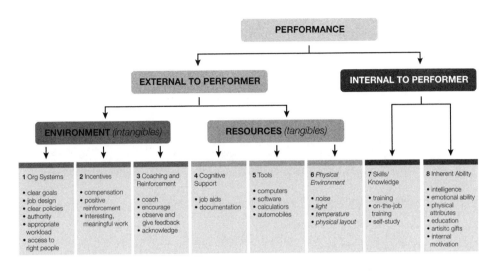

As you can see, individual performance and engagement hinges on multiple factors. What's holding back a change in behavior or improvement in performance? It could be the environment the employee is working in—misaligned systems, work processes, decision-making processes, or lack of feedback. It could be the employee doesn't have the resources he or she needs to implement the change, such as proper training, work space, or tools. Or it could be a lack of skill or will—the ability and motivation to do the job. Chances are, it's a combination of these factors, and that's where whole-systems thinking at the individual level becomes so critical. As a change leader, if you're not willing to understand the impact of each of these factors on the individual, then it's unlikely he or she is going to be willing to change behavior or improve performance.

...

**"You are a product of your environment.
So choose the environment that will best develop you
toward your objective. Analyze your life in terms of
its environment. Are the things around you helping you
toward success—or are they holding you back?"**

—Clement Stone, businessman and philanthropist

Though we don't expect you to become behavioral scientists, we want to help you identify what might hinder individual alignment so you can find solutions to move forward. Below are some simple questions we use to begin the conversation about individual alignment.

Questions to Enable Individual Alignment

- What will end and what will stay the same for employees?
- Why should they change?
- What's in it for them?
- What's the impact of not changing?
- What behaviors should employees stop, start, and continue doing?
- What's getting in the way of employees exhibiting the desired behaviors?
- What resources are needed?
- What new skills are required?
- Do employees have those skills? How can they obtain them if they don't have them?
- What's the "win" for the individual, team, and organization if they change?

THREE QUOTES SUMMARIZE THE IMPORTANCE OF INDIVIDUAL ALIGNMENT:

...

"He who has a *why* can endure any *how*."

—Friedrich Nietzsche, German philosopher

...

"The world hates change, yet it is the only thing that has brought progress."

—Charles F. Kettering, American inventor

...

"It is difficult to get a man to understand something when his salary depends upon his not understanding it."

—Upton Sinclair, American writer

When people know the *why* behind the change and have support mechanisms in place to enable new behavior, then they are more likely to align with the strategy of the organization. An example from one of our clients illustrates the risk of ignoring individual alignment in your change effort.

While working with a shipyard repair facility, we were struggling to get the sailors engaged when they interacted with frontline shipyard workers to repair the ships. We tried everything, but sailor engagement remained low. Out of frustration, one of the change team members went to where the sailors disembarked after a long work day and asked them a series of questions. What we discovered was surprising—engagement was low because the female sailors were unhappy. We found that work conditions for female sailors were different from those of their male counterparts. They told us there were no female restroom facilities within one and a half miles of the ship repair area. How could that be? In the United States, shipyards were built in the 1930s and 1940s. At that time, sailors were primarily male. Consequently, no one built female restrooms. After a dirty, hot day at work, women sailors had to trek across the shipyard to change, freshen up, or use the bathroom. In solidarity, male sailors weren't going to say things had improved if their female counterparts disagreed. Adding female restroom facilities closer to the repair area was relatively inexpensive and easy to do. Once that key individual need was met, the sailors were willing to engage in the more significant areas of change, and alignment surged forward.

Team Alignment

Individual alignment gets the change moving; team alignment gives it speed and direction. Organizations that effectively align teams to the change outperform other organizations at an accelerated rate. Look at the research from the article "The Hard Science of Teamwork." Sandy Pentland's team, from MIT's Human Dynamics Laboratory, gathered data about why some teams "click" or have a "buzz" about them when others don't. They asked team members to use wearable electronic sensors, and then they monitored the sensors to document how effective teams interact.[4] Below is a summary of their findings:

- **Communicate frequently.** A dozen or so communication exchanges per working hour is optimum (more or less than that and team performance can decline).

- **Talk and listen in equal measure, equally among members.** Lower-performing teams have dominant members, teams within teams, and members who talk or listen but don't do both.

- **Engage in frequent informal communication**. The best teams spend half their time communicating outside of formal meetings. Increasing opportunities for informal communication tends to increase team performance.

- **Explore ideas and information outside the group.** The best teams periodically connect with many different outside sources and bring what they learn back to the team.

According to Pentland's data, how "teams communicate turns out to be the most important predictor of team success, and *as important as all other factors combined,* including intelligence, personality, skill, and content of discussions." So powerful are these patterns of communication that they can predict how productive or creative a team will be. Pentland said, "Nothing will be more powerful, I believe, in eventually changing how organizations work."

For teams to get to this level of interaction, communication, and collaboration, they have to get two things right:

1. Create a climate within the team that is aligned and productive.

2. Align with other teams across boundaries to create sustainable solutions.

...

"Teamwork is the ability to work together toward a common vision; the ability to direct individual accomplishments toward organizational objectives. It is the fuel that allows common people to attain uncommon results."

—Andrew Carnegie, Scottish-American industrialist and philanthropist

1. Create an Aligned, Productive Climate Within the Team

Daniel Goleman conducted research significant to teams. He writes,

> We looked at the impact of climate on financial results—such as return on sales, revenue growth, efficiency, and profitability—[and] found a direct correlation between the two. Leaders who . . . positively affected the climate had decidedly better financial results than those who did not. That is not to say that organizational climate is the only driver of performance. But our analysis strongly suggests that climate accounts for nearly a third of results. And that's simply too much of an impact to ignore.[5]

We define climate as simply the culture of a particular team. For those who work in it, climate is almost invisible. It's the way things are done, what people do, or who people are. It is closely woven into the team's common vision of the future. Climate is composed of the values, assumptions, and mental models that are implicit within the way team members work. It includes the unwritten rules for how individuals work together, how the job gets done, acceptable styles, and approaches to solving problems. Climate is difficult to change because it's often transparent and varies from team to team. Our experience is that changing the climate within a team is difficult, but ultimately rewarding (worth 30% improvement in results). Be aware that when a change initiative requires a change in climate to be successful, it will require considerable alignment effort.

...

"People think of execution as the tactical side of the business, something leaders delegate while they focus on 'bigger' issues. This idea is completely wrong. Execution and sustaining results is the life-blood of a business; it has to be built into the fabric of the culture. That is the competitive advantage in change for business!"

—Larry Bossidy, former CEO, AlliedSignal

A team we worked with illustrates the power of climate in a team. One of our oil and gas clients was implementing SAP (systems, applications, and products) software in their purchasing and accounting processes. They had reassigned ten of their high-potential middle managers to work on the SAP project for two years. The plan was for these managers to become "super users"—individuals who had superior accounting skills and high proficiency in all aspects of the new SAP system. These super users were critical to the implementation of SAP in the business. They would act as the key help team for all employees during transition and training.

Two months before the "go live" date, the super users came to the SAP project manager and said, "We have loved our experience on this SAP project. The opportunity to work in a dynamic, collaborative team where there are both high expectations and high autonomy has been a unique work experience for us. We have decided that we are unwilling to go back to our old jobs if we have to work in our old, highly hierarchical system. Either redesign the process and system, or we will quit and find work elsewhere."[6]

The team climate these super users had come from wasn't conducive to the change that would happen, and they knew it.

The Ultimatum Game[7] is an interesting human experiment that highlights cultural differences between groups. Anthropologists have been playing this game with people from around the world to understand cultural differences in decision making. The game is played by bringing a group of people together and asking for two volunteers who will represent the culture of the group. The anthropologist shows the group a $100 bill. He explains to volunteer A that he is going to give him or her the money on one condition: he or she will have to share some of the money with volunteer B, and volunteer B must agree to the shared amount. If volunteer B doesn't accept the amount shared, neither volunteer A nor B gets any money. Volunteer A has only one chance to make an offer to volunteer B without talking or signaling to him or her in any way in advance.

What would you do if you were given the $100? From an economic standpoint, the perfect offer is to give volunteer B $1. Both will be better off than before. Volunteer A will have $99 more than before, and volunteer B will have $1 more. It's a win-win offer that volunteer B would be foolish to reject.

It's fascinating to see the results of the game in various cultures around the world. In Western cultures, volunteer A rarely makes the offer above. And when it's made, volunteer B almost always rejects it. Instead, Western offers are generally close to a 50/50 split. In contrast, volunteers from third-world cultures reject almost every offer, even highly favorable ones where volunteer A offers volunteer B almost all of the money. Why does this happen? What cultural assumptions are at play for people in Western cultures to act differently than people in third-world cultures?

In developed cultures, we have an assumption of fairness. Volunteer A feels a cultural obligation to be fair with this windfall and generally offers something close to a 50/50 split. When volunteer A does not do this, volunteer B will generally reject the offer because it violates the sense of fairness. In contrast, third-world cultures often have strong assumptions about gift giving and reciprocation. So volunteer B often rejects any offer because of the sense of obligation that he or she would have to reciprocate in the future.

Overlay this information onto organizations. Each team has a slightly different climate that comes with certain assumptions, and those assumptions will have a huge impact on how teams deal with change. An interview with a manager of a US transportation company illustrates the power of climate. The company was struggling to execute a merger because of strong cultural differences. The manager described it this way:

We are a rural, Southern-based company. We started in a small town, and our headquarters are still here.	They are urban, big city, East Coast people.
We drink beer and wear jeans.	They drink wine and wear suits.
When you work here, you are part of the family. You'd have to kill someone to get fired.	They are "up or out." You succeed quickly or you are let go.
We have few female managers and no female senior leaders.	They have lots of female leaders. It takes some getting used to in meetings.
On Sunday, we go to church.	On Sunday, they go to the beach if they aren't at the office.
We like to start business meetings with a prayer.	They look at us like we are crazy when we bow our heads.

But the power of climate doesn't just come from these visible clues, but what these clues tell you about the way people think, make decisions, and work together. Even the visible "artifacts" can seem invisible during day-to-day work, but most people can see the difference when they are given a good contrasting case. However, it takes a lot of skill to understand what these artifacts tell you about mental models and assumptions within a team.

The invisible nature of climate is what makes it so powerful. It is important to assess the change initiative in light of the current climate in the team. If the change initiative doesn't align with the current climate, then you must make one of two decisions:

1. Adjust the change initiative to align with the climate (use the power of the climate to help your change initiative succeed).

2. Incorporate climate modifications into your overall change initiative (the more difficult alternative, but necessary when climate is vastly misaligned with the change).

Many volumes have been written about getting team climate right (almost as much as about marriage, which gives you a clue as to the difficulty of getting relationships to work well). This section is not a complete treatise on teams. Instead, we want you to understand the importance of creating alignment at the team level by focusing on a few broad questions.

Questions to Enable Alignment within the Team

- What mental models and assumptions need to be updated to support the change?
- How does the team need to change the way it works to support the new results?
- What process changes will make work more effective?
- How can the team get the right people working together?
- How can the team make decisions more effectively?
- Who requires different skills, knowledge, experience, or motivation to do their jobs more effectively?
- What needs to change so that rewards drive desired behaviors?
- How can employees get needed information more quickly, accurately, and in the right format?

We remember several years ago when the management buzzword was teamwork. At the time, we worked in a corporation where we were told that if we collaborated as a team the solutions would be better and, ultimately, the results would be better. But the pay system didn't reward collaborative team behavior. It rewarded individual performance. At the end of the year, we were paid individually, as usual. So what did we do the next year? We talked a lot about teamwork, but continued to work individually. The compensation system simply wasn't aligned to support the new teamwork behavior. Similar misalignments happen over and over again, and leaders scratch their heads and wonder why they're not getting different results. The reason? They're not fixing alignment issues at the team level, so any progress that was made at the individual level comes to a screeching halt.

2. Align with Other Teams

Another important aspect of alignment is completing cross-functional checks with other groups and departments. Other teams have their own initiatives and changes that require time and resources. It's important to understand how your change will affect them and how their initiatives will impact the success of your change. Misalignment among teams can become a barrier to implementation if it's not adequately addressed.

One of our clients had a communication and operations dispatch center that had consolidated from fourteen local areas into one centralized, regional location. The transition was difficult and resulted in operational inefficiencies, cultural dysfunctions, and poor customer satisfaction. While the business case and the benefits for consolidation and standardization were clear and supported, the leadership team faced many other issues:

- Inadequate staffing ratios

- Inadequate skills to do the required jobs

- Uncompetitive pay

- Lack of standardized training

- No sense of urgency on behalf of the customer

- Little follow-through on promises

- A lack of partnering and collaboration between the field and centralized groups

After some analysis, the results proved dismal:

- **Employee turnover:** 40% (which prevented stability and effective execution)

- **Phone hold times for technicians**: Forty minutes (a technician's time on hold when calling from the customer's house to get access to certain system codes)

- **Overtime**: Significant increase (due to the unpredictable nature of the jobs)

- **Customer escalations**: Significant increase (which further complicated the scheduling and technical delivery processes)

- **Drive time between customer calls**: 1.5 times higher

- **Work order accuracy**: Worse (no support for technicians)

- **Employee morale**: All-time low

Because trust was low between all the groups and collaboration was scarce (it was every team for itself), the senior vice president over the region decided a cross-functional effort was necessary to solve the problems they were facing.

We can't overemphasize the importance of cross-functional collaboration to accelerate change. How many times have you seen independent teams create elegant, autonomous solutions that fail because they only worked in a vacuum? Organizations aren't vacuums; they are organic, interdependent entities. Given the complexity of problems facing organizations today, teams must work together to generate sustainable solutions. Creating alignment means balancing interests, resources, accountability, schedules, and results—among all teams. You figure out what they need from you and what you need from them to successfully implement the change. Completing these cross-functional checks is the only way to implement successful solutions that will fix the business.

For our regionalized dispatch center, cross-functional collaboration was a key turning point for them. Every week the teams had to report on their progress, discuss issues, and coordinate how and when they would work together on solutions. Joint accountability for the success of the project improved morale, reduced turnover, enabled collaboration, and increased customer satisfaction across the region. Implementation of ideas happened quickly given the coordination between teams. And they began to realize the desired results from regionalization that caused them to make the change in the first place.

Below are some questions we use to surface misalignments *between* teams. You'll notice that many of them are the same questions we use to create alignment *within* teams.

Questions to Enable Alignment between Teams

- What other parts of the business will be impacted by this change?
- How do we get their buy-in for the change?
- How can we work together to implement change?
- What process changes will make work more effective?
- How can we get the right people working together?
- How can we make decisions more effectively?
- Who requires different skills, knowledge, experience, or motivation to do their jobs more effectively?
- What measures need to change to track progress and enable joint accountability?
- How do rewards need to be aligned to share ownership?
- How can people get needed information more quickly, accurately, and in the right format?

Organizational Alignment

In addition to overlooking the need for individual and team alignment in change, leaders often overlook the need for organizational alignment because of the perceived complexity. But change leaders need to be aware of the powerful impact that business processes, systems, structures, and culture have on behavior change. When these organizational elements aren't aligned, change doesn't happen.

As an example, let's assume that you were recently promoted and acquired an underperforming business unit that already existed within your organization. In your first ninety days, you would likely conduct a thorough analysis of what's working and what's not. If the organization isn't performing to expectations, and knowing that "organizations are perfectly designed to get the results they get," you'd likely conduct a diagnostic of the misalignments and identify areas for improvement. In your organizational analysis, you might ask the following questions:

Questions to Diagnose Organizational Alignment

- How is the organization set up today?
- How satisfied are stakeholders (customers, funders, users, employees)?
- What are the current results? What are the desired results? How big is the gap?
- What's the culture like? What behaviors contribute to positive results? What behaviors contribute to poor performance?
- Are the priorities on which people are focused consistent across the business?
- How do the processes, structure, and systems contribute to positive behavior? How do they contribute to inconsistent behavior and poor results?
- How clear are the mission and vision of the organization?
- Are the values believed, lived, and reinforced?
- Is the strategy clear? Are employees and teams aligned with the strategy?

These types of questions would help you get a feel for where you'd need to make adjustments in your newly acquired business unit. But to really understand the dynamics and complexities of the organization, you'd have to dive deeper, using a model called the Organizational Effectiveness (OE) Cycle.[8]

The OE Cycle is a tool that helps leaders understand how all of the elements in their organization are aligned to enable performance. It facilitates systemic thinking (i.e., viewing the organization as an ecosystem rather than just a collection of pieces), and it illustrates the interdependent relationships between the key organizational elements. The OE Cycle can clarify cause-and-effect factors that impact results. Additionally, it can be used to identify key leverage points—those few elements that could improve the organization's overall performance.

Organizational Effectiveness Cycle

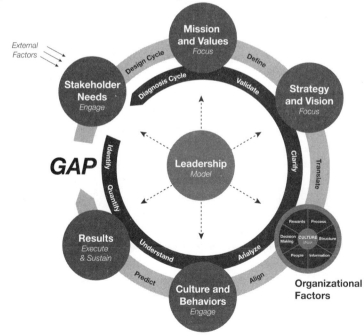

Adapted from Franklin Covey's Organizational Effectiveness Cycle

More often than not, leaders tinker with one or two of these organizational elements without understanding the impact of their actions on the total system. Such tinkering can thrust a stable system out of control and create poor performance. When leaders understand that "all organizations are perfectly designed (or aligned) to get the results they get," they can focus on all elements and create a balanced design of mission, strategy, processes, and culture. The OE Cycle can be used to diagnose organizational alignment, design organizational alignment, or both.

The Diagnosis Cycle

To get to the root of any issue, Dr. Edwards Deming counseled leaders to ask the 5 Whys mentioned earlier in this chapter. The underlying questions of "Why?" and "What is contributing to our current results?" are present during each step. The diagnosis process begins with the "Stakeholder Needs" in the cycle, and then moves counterclockwise.[9]

Step 1	**Stakeholder Needs:** Identify stakeholders—all those who have an important "stake" in the success of the organization. Having a "stake" means they have a primary need that your organization can fulfill. Stakeholders could be employees, other organizations or groups, vendors, government/regulatory agencies, funders, and customers. Environmental factors can have a major impact on the health of the organization and should also be considered. A good diagnosis defines the needs—both now and in the future—of the most critical stakeholders.
Step 2	**Results:** Define the results, including areas of excellence and incompetence, based on stakeholder needs. Quantify, "How well are we meeting each of our key stakeholder needs? Where are the gaps between what they need and what we are delivering?" The size of the gap will inform the extent of change required.

Step 3	**Culture and Behaviors:** Understand current results by identifying the work behaviors and patterns that critically influence results. These behaviors and patterns make up the culture of the organization—the collection of observable, individual behaviors that routinely occur. As we noted earlier, a subculture or climate may exist for a defined part of the organization (e.g., sales, education, media), different hierarchical levels (e.g., senior executives, middle managers, supervisors, employees), or other intangible but real divisions (e.g., line vs. staff, headquarters vs. field, local vs. foreign, etc.). Culture is what the vast majority of people actually do most of the time.
Step 4	**Organizational Factors:** Analyze the organizational factors that enable the current cultural behaviors to occur. The organizational factors (or infrastructure) you create (consciously or unconsciously, well-designed or haphazardly) act to nurture, sustain, and encourage the observable behaviors of the majority of people the majority of the time. If the mass of people behave (or don't behave) some particular way the vast majority of the time, it is because some organizational factor (or combination of factors) currently exists that creates, sustains, nurtures, and encourages that behavioral pattern. If leaders intend to change the culture, they must identify and align the organizational factors (e.g., work processes, structure, roles and responsibilities, rewards, information, decision making, technology, and performance management) that will enable the desired behaviors.
Step 5	**Strategy and Vision:** Clarify employee understanding of the strategy and vision, including the impact they are having on results. Determine the extent that strategy and vision are contributing to focus: • **Strategy:** The fundamental approach to gaining competitive advantage in the marketplace • **Vision:** The collective idea about where the business is trying to go—the direction for the future

Step 6

Mission and Values: Validate how the mission and values of the organization are enforced or abandoned and the impact on current results. The clarity of the mission and values in the individual and collective minds of employees in the organization can lead to focus and alignment or confusion and poor execution.

- **Mission:** The individual and collective idea about the purpose of the organization
- **Values:** The overarching code of conduct—how people will treat each other as they work to accomplish the mission

Step 7

Leadership: To better understand the ultimate root cause of business performance, determine the individual and collective leadership effectiveness of senior leaders. Leaders who are ineffective have a direct, negative correlation to business results. Aggregate leadership effectiveness (or ineffectiveness) can lead to growth and scalability or poor performance and decline. Determine in this step if leaders are focused and aligned across the organization; if beliefs, assumptions, and patterns of behavior are at odds with each other; if leadership effectiveness is emphasized; and if developmental efforts are yielding a Return on Investment. Leaders who are controlling, autocratic, overly ambitious, and critical (to name just a few) stifle creativity, team play, and engagement—all critical factors needed to accelerate change. This step is about understanding what is holding the organization back from increasing individual leadership capacity and evolving leadership team effectiveness. This is rarely the focus of most transformation efforts and consequently results in unsustainable performance improvement. Change experts Bob Anderson and Bill Adams have found that "the number one reason for failure of strategy is not that is was poorly conceived. It is because the collective leadership effectiveness to execute that strategy is inadequate."[10]

Careful diagnosis will help change leaders understand behaviors, processes, and systems that are enabling great performance or producing poor results. This understanding will help leaders become systemic thinkers as they move into the design cycle.

The Design Cycle

When designing a high-performance business, leaders work clockwise through the OE Cycle, starting again with "Stakeholder Needs" to ensure the organization is aligned to deliver what stakeholders want. The design cycle can be summarized as follows:

Steps 1–3	Define the mission, values, vision, and strategy to better focus the organization to deliver customer and other stakeholder needs.
Step 4	Translate the priorities of the mission, values, vision, and strategy so that employees can align the organizational factors to deliver on those imperatives. Note: if one organizational factor is changed, the other factors at least need to be reviewed (and likely changed) to ensure alignment.
Step 5	Align the organizational factors to enable the desired cultural behaviors that will deliver great results. An effective way to do this is to summarize the FROM→TO behaviors that everyone in the organization needs to stop and start doing.
Step 6	Predict the results that will be produced by this new culture and behaviors of leaders. If the predicted results still fall short of stakeholder needs, then revisit steps 1–5 and adjust the design as needed.

Alignment of Organizational Factors

Aligning organizational factors (step 5) is probably the most challenging step to get right. Let's take a deeper dive into each component that makes up this step. The following questions will help leaders collectively discuss and then design more effective and efficient processes and systems that will improve the performance of the business.

- **Process**: The step-by-step flow of work; it is how things get done day to day. Key questions:
  - What work needs to be done?
  - What changes will be required to how people do work?
  - What new work needs to be added?
  - What work no longer needs to be done?
  - Have any output requirements changed?

- **Structure**: The way work processes are organized, which includes reporting relationships, roles and responsibilities, and accountabilities. Key questions:
  - How does the work need to be organized?
  - Which roles need to be clarified in this new design? What are the responsibilities, accountabilities, and level of authority for each role?
  - Who needs to work together to accomplish the work?
  - What are the most appropriate reporting relationships?

- **Information**: The system that enables how information is tracked, reported, and communicated to people; in other words, getting the right information to the right people at the right time. Key questions:
  - How will information requirements change?
  - Who needs what information? In what format? By when?
  - How will people get the information in a timely fashion?
  - How will process results be tracked, measured, and reported?

- **People**: The system that facilitates how people are attracted, selected, oriented, trained, certified, performance managed, and developed. Key questions:
  - What capabilities are required to do the work?
  - What new behaviors are required?
  - What are the development needs to implement the work processes?
  - What are the staffing needs to implement the work processes?
  - What implications do the work processes have on how people will be attracted, selected, oriented, developed, certified, evaluated, and promoted in the organization?

- **Decision Making**: The process that clarifies who has authority to do the work and how decisions are made. Key questions:
  - Is the authority to make decisions clear?
  - Has the work been designed so decisions are made at the lowest possible level?
  - Who needs what authority to make better and faster decisions?
  - What needs to change so the right people are consulted on decisions?
  - Can people get approval without encountering excessive bureaucracy?

- **Rewards**: The system designed to acknowledge and compensate individuals for their contributions. Key questions:
  - How will people be valued?
  - What behaviors should be rewarded in the new work processes?
  - How should individuals, teams, and groups be recognized for good work?
  - Which intrinsic satisfiers would enable the implementation of the new work processes (e.g., personal growth, professional challenge, autonomy, achievement, responsibility, interaction with colleagues, meaningful work, interaction with leaders, and recognition)?

- **Technology**: The equipment, technology, facilities, and furniture that enable the work to get done. Key questions:
  - How will technology shift?
  - What are the logistical and work space needs of the different work processes?
  - Do workers have effective communication technology?
  - Do people have the equipment and technology (hardware and software) they need to complete the work processes?
  - Is there plenty of meeting space (physical and virtual) to enable collaboration?

Let's return to the example of your promotion to an underper-forming business unit. Given your analysis of the issues that are helping and hindering organizational effectiveness in your new role, you recognize that focusing on only a few factors will not ensure a high-performing organization. You realize that to design an aligned organization, you need to look at both effectiveness of people and efficiency of the organization. You need to define the desired culture in terms of people's attitudes, behaviors, and beliefs. You need to involve those doing the work (those who know best) in designing and aligning the organizational infrastructure. And you need to improve the individual and collective leadership effectiveness of the business (see chapter 5, Accelerating Leadership).

John Gardner said, "Most ailing organizations have developed a functional blindness to their own defects. They are not suffering because they cannot resolve their problems, but because they cannot see their problems." While many in the organization have a sense that performance isn't what it should be, the OE Cycle helps leaders *see* misalignments that are contributing to poor results and *know* what organizational elements they need to change to produce great results that exactly meet stakeholder needs.

One of our clients discovered how critical organizational align-ment is to accelerate change. This client is in the home improvement business. For simplicity, let's assume our client was considering two different strategic approaches to meet customer needs: (1) a prod-uct-focused company with a retail store delivery model, and (2) a solu-tion-focused company with a multi-channel delivery model. Assume both strategies have the intent to make the customer experience great. To see how a change leader must align all of the organizational factors, let's walk through a typical home improvement scenario—redoing a kitchen—and apply each strategy.

In a product-focused company, the physical layout of the retail store is organized by product. So a customer might enter the store and start in the cabinet or appliance section and then move through the paint, flooring, and lighting sections to create a coordinated new look and feel for the redesign of the kitchen. In this model, the work processes are functionally focused (e.g., sourcing paint is a separate process from sourcing cabinets), and the structure of the store is organized by product.

In a solution-focused company, this strategy creates a different customer experience. A customer might enter the store and go to the kitchen section that has all the flooring, paint, appliances, and cabinets needed for kitchen remodels. The store could have similar one-stop-shop sections for a bathroom upgrade or outdoor patio. The customer could choose to do a lot of shopping and planning online, while sourcing some items through the Internet and other items onsite at the retail location. In this model, the merchandising managers would no longer create formal vertical plans for their merchandise product area. Instead, the merchandising process would be integrated with other functional areas to enable the total customer experience.

Both strategies work as long as the organizational alignment supports the strategy. Our client decided to change from a product-focused approach to a solution-focused approach because it seemed to create more interest and excitement for stakeholders. Merely restructuring the company wasn't enough. They had to intentionally look at each system and make changes to support the new strategy.

...

"Any time the majority of the people behave a particular way the majority of the time, the people are not the problem. The problem is inherent in the system."

—W. Edwards Deming, author and quality expert

A BlessingWhite study summarized this concept:

> Despite leadership rhetoric about employees having "line of sight" to organizational goals and the power of organizational score-cards, many employees remain in the dark about how their daily priorities fit in with their employer's objectives. Alignment is the missing link for employees who want to do work that matters, belong to something of consequence, and achieve greatness with their talents.[11]

LEADER CAUTION!

Before you get discouraged or overwhelmed with the thought of alignment, remember that we're not asking you to be organizational effectiveness experts. If the processes, structure, or systems need major realignment, call in professionals who can help. But at a minimum, ask yourself two questions:

1. What are the requirements of each of these organizational factors to enable the change we want?
2. What needs to be designed, aligned, or fit together to execute the change?

...

**"Changing the system will change what people do.
Changing what people do will not change the system."**

—Peter Scholtes, author

Based on your responses to these questions, you can determine the level of support you need from internal and external resources to make the change happen. Alignment work is not simple, but using a systemic model, such as the OE Cycle, and working methodically through each system will create rewarding work and bottom-line results.

CONCLUSION

Michael Porter, one of the most well-known organizational strategists, said, "Competitive advantage grows out of the *entire system* of activities. . . . Strategic fit among many activities is fundamental not only to competitive advantage but also to the sustainability of that advantage. Positions built on systems of activities are far more sustainable than those built on individual activities."[12]

"Strategic fit" in change is aligning the organization to deliver results. It's a lot like changing the tire on a car. If you watch any good mechanic change a tire, you'll see they follow a systematic process for tightening the lug nuts equally. If that equalizing process doesn't happen, you'll feel the car vibrate or shake at high speeds, which is bumpy at best and terrifying at worst.

The same is true with change. If leaders try to shortcut the process of creating alignment among each of the systems, the change is going to be unpleasant at best and a complete failure at worst. Both the efficiency and effectiveness of the organization will be compromised. Accelerating change in an organization requires leaders to intentionally define and align those activities that set the organization apart and give it a competitive edge at the individual, team, and organizational levels.

CHAPTER SUMMARY

KEY POINTS

- "Organizations are perfectly designed to get the results they get."

- Change leaders must become organizational architects able to diagnose what is inhibiting the right behaviors in an organization and then design solutions that are aligned in a way to support long-term, sustainable results.

- Holistic design is the most overlooked accelerator of change among senior leaders. Unless business leaders look at the entirety of their operations and align all systems to work together, the organization won't become a high-performance business.

- When leaders inspire individuals to align their behaviors with the new direction of the organization, those individuals will collectively make a difference. This is not to suggest that you *change* people. Instead, the first alignment leaders need to get right is to help people align their passion and energies with the direction of the change initiative. If a leader is not willing to understand the impact of all the factors of change on employees, then it's unlikely those employees will be willing to change behavior or improve performance.

- When people know the *why* behind the change and have support mechanisms in place to enable new behavior, then they are more likely to align themselves with the change initiative.

- Individual alignment gets the change moving; team alignment gives it speed and direction. Organizations that effectively align teams to the change outperform other organizations at an accelerated rate.

- Given the complexity of problems facing organizations today, it's critical to get teams working together to generate sustainable solutions. Creating alignment means balancing interests, resources, accountability, schedules, and results—among all teams.

- More often than not, leaders tinker with one or two organizational elements without understanding the impact of their actions on the total system. Such tinkering can thrust a stable system out of control and create poor performance.

- If the mass of employees behave (or don't behave) a particular way the vast majority of the time, it is because some organizational factor (or combination of factors) currently exists that creates, sustains, nurtures, and encourages that behavioral pattern. If leaders intend to change the organization, they must identify the organizational factors (e.g., work processes, structure, roles and responsibilities, rewards, information, decision making, technology, and performance management) that are driving the cultural behaviors.

- Accelerating change in an organization requires leaders to intentionally define and align those activities that set the organization apart and give it a competitive edge at the individual, team, and organizational levels.

ACCELERATING ENGAGEMENT

"Faced with the choice between changing one's mind
and proving that there is no need to do so, almost
everybody gets busy on the proof."

—John Kenneth Galbraith, American economist

On January 28, 1986, seventy-three seconds into its flight, the *Challenger* space shuttle disaster occurred. Technical reason? The O-ring seals. On February 1, 2003, the space shuttle *Columbia* disaster happened as the shuttle disintegrated upon reentering the atmosphere. Technical reason? A suitcase-sized piece of thermal insulation foam broke off from the external tank and struck *Columbia*'s left wing reinforced carbon-carbon (RCC) panels. The two disasters led to a lack of public confidence in NASA and a reduction in funding. After rigorous research into the issues related to these two incidents, the *Columbia* Accident Investigation Board (CAIB) issued its findings. The report concluded that NASA's organizational culture had as much to do with the *Columbia* accident as technical failure. According to the report, cultural and organizational practices detrimental to safety were allowed to develop within NASA. One of the major recommendations of the CAIB report was to completely transform NASA's organizational and safety culture. So in September 2004 the NASA Kennedy Space Center put out a Request for Proposal (RFP) soliciting help with the transformation. The charge was for NASA to make measurable progress in changing its culture within six months, demonstrate significant transformation within one year, and make broad changes across the agency within three years.

With a change project of this size, the RFP attracted many bidders, including us. We had done some previous project work at the Kennedy Space Center, so we were excited about the possibility of leveraging that knowledge in a bigger culture and change project. We spent weeks preparing a proposal and making a presentation to the contracting officers. We were confident we would get a callback to present to senior leadership. We waited with anticipation, but no callback came. We had lost the bid—no request for more information, no callback to present our brilliant plan, no explanation other than a "thank you."

Early in 2005, we found out more about the consulting firm that won the contract and their solution. To solve the underlying cultural and organizational issues, they put everyone through a half-day training about change management. *That* was the remedy to fix decades of culture issues? We were shocked. How could we lose to that? Our plan included many of the things described in this book—it was a holistic, inside-out/outside-in approach that integrated strategy and organizational alignment with culture change. And yet, we were on the outside looking in. (Disclaimer: There might have been more to the winning firm's plan, but that was all we were told.)

Step away for a minute from the NASA situation and think about the most perplexing issues facing your organization. Ask yourself these questions:

- Are the issues relatively simple or complex?

- Can the problems be solved by fixing just one area of the organization or many?

- Are the fundamental problems caused primarily by organizational barriers or people behaviors?

- Does everyone agree on the solution(s)?

- Why haven't these issues been fixed previously?

If the difficult issues you face are anything like those faced by most organizations, simple and quick-fix solutions (like putting everyone through a training course) aren't going to create sustainable change. A few senior leaders at the Kennedy Space Center came to this same conclusion, to their credit, and initiated four key improvement initiatives as part of the broader change project. The four initiatives focused on (1) leadership communication, (2) performance management and development, (3) engineering/technical improvement, and (4) values implementation. They were designed to address deep-rooted culture and process issues within the center that had formed over a long period of time and required a high level of focus, attention, and expertise to fix.

Though we had lost the larger deal, we were asked to partner with the Change Manager who was accountable for implementing the four initiatives. As we worked with him, we were again reminded of how difficult it can be to change. Edwin Shneidman, pioneer in the field of suicide prevention, said, "If you listen for hurt, fear, and pain, or for people's hopes and dreams, it is nearly always there. And when the other person feels you listening and feeling them, they will let down their guard and open their minds and hearts to you." Unfortunately, the culture at NASA did not inspire this type of open, honest communication. For the most part, the problems that caused the *Challenger* and *Columbia* accidents were known. Some solutions to the problems had even surfaced, but because of cultural, scheduling, and political pressures, they were overlooked.

...

"People don't resist change. They resist being changed."

—Peter Senge, American systems scientist

THE MILLION-DOLLAR QUESTION

So if NASA knew about the problems and even had some solutions, why didn't they change? It's a question we get asked a lot—if people know *what* to do, *why* don't they do it? As we know, many things create the gap between knowing and doing. Does your teenager know what a clean room looks like? More than likely. So why doesn't she keep her room clean to that standard? Do you know you should eat right, get enough sleep, and exercise regularly? Probably. So why don't you do it? In our personal and business lives, we all live with the gap between knowing what to do and actually doing it.

Let's try a simple exercise to prove the point.

- Step 1: Sit down in a chair away from a table.

- Step 2: Extend your right leg and make circles with your right foot in a clockwise direction.

- Step 3: While keeping your right foot rotating clockwise, draw a number six in the air with your right index finger.

Can you do it? Can you keep your foot rotating clockwise while drawing a number six in the air with your right hand? What if someone cheered you on? Would that help? What if we offered you a promotion? What if we increased your pay? The reality is that none of those things would help most people. Most of us are hardwired to *not* be able to do this simple exercise.

Now try this. Follow steps 1 and 2 above. For step 3, use your right index finger to draw a six starting on the inside of the bottom circle and tracing it in the reverse direction. Can you now keep your foot rotating clockwise while drawing a number six in the air with your right index finger? More than likely you can.

In the first exercise, you knew what to do, but most likely you couldn't do it. Why? Was it lack of skill, desire, motivation? In an article called "Fast and Effective Change Management," Phillip Ash describes the typical approach to change as "simply announce what the changes will be and expect everyone to comply." How often does that approach work? It has the same success rate as our little exercise. People know what to do, but that doesn't mean they do it.

Some employees have had negative experiences in the past with change. Some don't understand how they will be impacted, or they feel uncertain about the future. And others might mourn the per-ceived "loss" caused by the change. As Ash observed, employees are creatures of habit and aren't always willing to expend the large measure of discretionary effort that is usually required to change. So for multiple reasons, when a change is announced employees often resist. It's like rotating your foot and drawing a six—it's awkward and hard and some people just don't want to change (while others might not be able to change).

Change leaders must work through and neutralize the natural resistance to doing something different. People need information and support to successfully navigate the transitions required to trans-form the business. Accelerating engagement is the ultimate driver for change sponsors to get better results. Nothing is so powerful as unleashing the passion and energy of employees toward change. You won't have to nag, cajole, bribe, plead, or bargain to get them to go above and beyond. They will willingly do it themselves.

In his insightful book *Epic Change*, our colleague Tim Clark wrote, "To lead change is nothing less than to summon and redirect institutional will and capacity."[1] Accelerating engagement by summoning and redirecting will and capacity requires three factors:

1. Overcoming resistance

2. Managing transitions

3. Enabling greater engagement

These factors are independent and interdependent as they build upon each other. Let's look at each one in turn to understand the components of accelerating engagement.

...

"Nothing is so dear as what you're about to leave."

—Jessamyn West, American writer

Factor 1: Overcoming Resistance

In a study by the Conference Board, respondents rated organizational resistance as the biggest challenge to implementing successful change.[2] Resistance is a natural reaction to any change. For example, employees have been trained to work in a particular way, they follow certain processes, and they have mastered those processes over time. Then a change comes along. Isn't it natural that at least some people would question the change even when the reasons are compelling? Others might go beyond questioning and simply refuse to budge. Psychologists and motivational theorists shed light on why people resist. At the most basic level, resistance to change is a breakdown in what we call the Commitment Curve. Any change requires people to move through the curve from Unawareness on the left to Commitment on the right, with all of the other phases in between. Different people will be at different places on the curve when change is announced. If they are on the left side of the curve, their resistance will be greater. If they are on the right side of the curve, their resistance will be less.

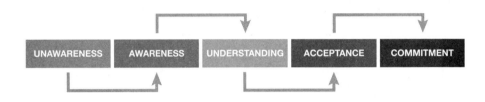

In the **Unawareness Phase**, an employee typically won't know anything about the need for change. Announcing the change helps, but they usually need more than a memo, presentation, or email. In the **Awareness Phase**, employees know the basic facts about the change and the plan for implementation. It's not until the **Understanding Phase** that most employees start to realize why the change is important and how it will impact their work as well as their coworkers and customers. However, understanding is still a long way from **Acceptance** where employees actually buy in to the change and are willing to give it a try. Finally, the **Commitment Phase** is when employees and leaders alike are passionate and energized about the change. Their desire for a better future state outweighs the need for the comfort of the status quo.

An example from our client work illustrates the importance of understanding the Commitment Curve. Several years ago, we had a senior leader of a company struggling to get the buy-in he felt was needed to make a significant change in the direction of the business. We interviewed many of the other senior leaders as well as employees, and it was obvious they weren't on the same page about the change.

We shared our findings with the senior leader who became very frustrated (almost angry) with us. We asked him how many times he had shared his vision of the change. He said twice—once in a general discussion with senior leaders, and once in a fifteen-minute presentation to senior managers followed by fifteen minutes of questions and answers. That was it? What seemed obvious to us wasn't obvious to him. He asked us multiple times, "Why don't they get it?"

Before we get too critical of this leader, put yourself in his shoes. Had he spent significant time thinking about, studying, brooding over, and discussing the situation with a few confidants? Yes. Did he have data to support his position? Yes. And in this case, his back was against the wall—change had to happen or the business wouldn't survive. What we had him do was put himself in his employees' shoes. Had *they* spent significant time wrestling with the issues facing the business? No. They were too busy running the day-to-day operation. Did they have access to the same data? No. Had they realized the critical condition of the business? Not really. The senior leader was on the far right of the Commitment Curve and his employees were on the far left. He expected them to complete the full cycle and work through all of their questions, concerns, doubts, anxieties, and fears after only one fifteen-minute presentation.

Understanding the Commitment Curve, and assessing where employees are on the curve, can help you anticipate the level of resistance to change and plan ways to overcome it. We use a simple tool called Head, Hands, Heart to accelerate the pace at which people arrive at the Commitment Phase. **Head** activities (e.g., electronic communication, live meetings, memos, etc.) emphasize facts, logic, and details. When you engage the head, you answer questions about the rationale of the change—the why, what, when, where, how, and who. Leaders engage the **Hands** of employees by orienting them to the new skills and capabilities required, letting them try it out, and rewarding people for experimenting. Engaging the hands allows employees to pilot the new system before "going live" and to see how it will improve their work. Leaders know they are making progress along the Commitment Curve when employees are confident that they have the skills to perform the new work required of them.

Engaging the **Heart** is often more difficult than the head and hands. Leaders tend to shy away from addressing the emotional side of change. They're uncomfortable and untrained in dealing with emotions at work. But emotion and passion is the powerful fuel that will ignite and accelerate change! Don't miss the opportunity to engage the hearts of your people. Here are just a few activities that can help:

- Describe why the change is important.

- Share "What's in it for me?"

- Describe how the change will impact friends and trusted colleagues.

- Summarize the benefits to customers and suppliers.

- Engage employees in the assessment of the problem(s).

- Delegate responsibility and ownership for change.

- Keep score; hold people accountable; show improvement.

- Share positive feedback about what's improving.

- Celebrate small wins.

- Make convincing decisions that show you are serious about the change.

- Provide learning opportunities.

- Give people a chance to develop new relationships in small teams.

- Show the potential impact on performance and value of the change.

- Aim for a realistic amount of change.

- Say "no" to what the organization will no longer do.

While this list isn't exhaustive, it can help you engage the hearts of your people. American futurist Marilyn Ferguson said, "It's not so much that we're afraid of change or so in love with the old ways, but it's that place in between that we fear. . . . It's like being between trapezes. It's Linus when his blanket is in the dryer. There's nothing to hold on to." By engaging the head, hands, and heart, you are giving employees the courage they need to let go of the old, embrace the new, and commit to doing things differently.

...

"The crisis consists precisely in the fact that the old is dying and the new cannot be born. In this interregnum, a great variety of morbid symptoms appear."

—Antonio Gramsci, Italian political activist

Other elements important to overcoming resistance were summarized by Kathleen D. Dannemiller in what has become known as the Change Formula.[3] Dannemiller's equation postulates that for change to be successful, dissatisfaction multiplied by vision multiplied by first steps must be greater than resistance.

The Change Equation

For change to be successful, the product of three factors—level of dissatisfaction with the status quo, the new vision of what is possible, and the practical first steps to change—has to be greater than the resistance to change (both financial and emotional).

Source: Dannemiller Tyson Associates

Let's take a look at each component. First, there must be a sufficient level of **dissatisfaction** with the status quo to create a readiness for change. If dissatisfaction is low or nonexistent, resistance to change will likely be high. Dissatisfaction might be caused by lack of growth in the business, poor business performance, loss of customers, not enough opportunities, or lack of collaboration.

Second, leaders must establish a clear **vision** for the change, which we addressed in previous chapters. Our former colleague Jim Stuart used to say that the vision of the desired future must be compelling enough to get people off their "buts," meaning that people have a tendency to say, "But what about ... ?" or "But can't I continue to ... ?" or "But why should we ... ?" When people can envision a desired future they want to be a part of (and no longer say "But what about ... ?"), resistance can be overcome. Vision could include a new value proposition, a desired business growth rate, or success in new markets.

Third, the change must have practical **first steps** that employees believe will help achieve the vision. Steps must include what leaders are going to do to help the business get better, stronger, and more competitive. The product of these three variables must be greater than the natural **resistance** inherent in any system (organizationally or individually) for change to succeed.

It's important to note the multiplicative relationship between each of these factors in the change equation. In other words, it is not enough to have just one or two—it usually takes the combined force of all three to have enough strength to overcome resistance.

...

**"All changes, even the most longed for, have their melancholy;
for what we leave behind is part of ourselves; we must die
to one life before we can enter into another."**

—Anatole France, French writer

Tools of the Trade

Traditional change management methodology is replete with tools change leaders can use to overcome resistance. We want to mention just a few that you should be comfortable with as you lead and manage change.

- **Stakeholder Analysis and Engagement**. Stakeholder analysis includes identifying (typically on a bell curve) the natural distribution of innovators, early adopters, early majority, late majority, laggards, and immovables. It also maps stakeholder groups by name and summarizes their needs. Without detailing everything involved in stakeholder analysis and engagement, we recommend the following three activities at a minimum:

  ○ Identify all stakeholders
  ○ Predict the impact of the change on stakeholders
  ○ Determine actions necessary to secure stakeholder commitment

- **Communication Planning and Events**. A lot has been written about communication, and we encourage you to study the literature. At the basic level, smart leaders of change communicate with employees in a way that resembles open, transparent person-to-person conversation rather than a series of directives. To start and maintain a friendly dialogue about change, you need a strong communication plan, which includes deadlines and milestones. A simple tool we use to ensure consistent messaging that we learned from our colleague Jim Dowling is called the 3-30-3-30 method. The idea is that your communication should have four formats with uniform messaging:

  ○ 3-second message—typically 3 words
  ○ 30-second message—typically 3 sentences that describe the 3 words

- 3-minute message—typically 3 paragraphs that expound on the 3 sentences
- 30-minute message—typically a PowerPoint presentation that includes all the details of the change plan

We experimented with this tool when we helped a pharmaceutical manufacturing company transition ten of its fifteen plants to a just-in-time inventory system. During the project, we were having trouble communicating consistent messages about the change to all stakeholders. The 3-30-3-30 tool helped crystalize the message into useful formats and eliminate confusion about what was happening. It was so successful that we use this tool with all of our clients now.

- **Involvement Strategies**. You've heard the saying "No involvement, no commitment." Consequently, we use a number of strategies to involve as many people as we can at each phase of the project. We use surveys, focus groups, and interviews. We hold town hall meetings, place people on assessment and change teams, and have "war room" review sessions. If you can't formally involve as many people as you want in your change initiative, ask them these questions instead:
  - What are you most afraid of?
  - What will it take to get the change implemented?
  - What will get in your way?
  - How can we make it as painless as possible?

And remember the golden rule of change: Don't do to them what you wouldn't want done to you!

...

**"Many a man would rather you heard his story
than granted his request."**

–Philip Stanhope, Earl of Chesterfield

Factor 2: Managing Transitions

If identifying dissatisfaction with the status quo, clarifying the vision, and planning the first steps isn't tricky enough, managing the emotions people experience during change can feel overwhelming. When people are asked to change their skills, behaviors, or attitudes, they will naturally respond at a deeply emotional level. These emotional responses vary based on whether a person views the change as beneficial or not. But in any case, as the change unfolds, people will begin to experience the ramifications of the change and will move through a cycle of emotional responses (usually at different rates, depending on the person). Helping people transition through negative emotional responses to positive ones as quickly as possible accelerates the rate of the change. William Bridges, a leading author in organizational change, addresses the issue of transitions this way:

> It isn't the changes that do you in, it's the transitions. Change is not the same as transition. *Change* is situational: the new site, the new boss, the new team roles, the new policy. *Transition* is the psychological process people go through to come to terms with the new situation. Change is external, transition is internal. . . . Situational change hinges on the new thing, but psychological transition depends on letting go of the old reality and the old identity you had before the change took place. . . . Once you understand that *transition begins with letting go of something*, you have taken the first step in the task of transition management.[4]

Unless psychological transition takes place, the proposed organizational change will not succeed. Bridges found that "the failure to identify and be ready for the endings and losses that change produces is the largest single problem that organizations in transition encounter."[5] And it's those endings and losses that make transition so difficult. Sir Henry Taylor, an English dramatist, poet, and official, wisely said, "He that lacks time to mourn, lacks time to mend." Managing the emotional cycle of change enables employees to mourn, mend, and ultimately transition to the new state of things.

The Emotional Cycle of Change below[6] is based on a model that was first introduced by Swiss psychiatrist Elisabeth Kübler-Ross in her 1969 book *On Death and Dying*, and was inspired by her work with terminally ill patients. She found five stages of grief, or a series of emotions, experienced by terminally ill patients prior to death. She later expanded her theory to apply to any form of personal loss, such as the death of a loved one, the loss of a job or income, the end of a relationship, the onset of a disease, or any other tragedy. Many change agents have found a parallel between change and death. While change shouldn't be as dramatic as losing a loved one, the endings and losses can have a strong emotional impact on employees.

The Emotional Cycle of Change

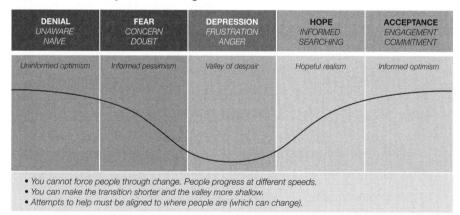

DENIAL UNAWARE NAÏVE	FEAR CONCERN DOUBT	DEPRESSION FRUSTRATION ANGER	HOPE INFORMED SEARCHING	ACCEPTANCE ENGAGEMENT COMMITMENT
Uninformed optimism	Informed pessimism	Valley of despair	Hopeful realism	Informed optimism

- You cannot force people through change. People progress at different speeds.
- You can make the transition shorter and the valley more shallow.
- Attempts to help must be aligned to where people are (which can change).

The first stage of change people experience is **Uninformed Optimism**. In this stage, they exhibit initial enthusiasm, high expectations, and confidence in their ability to deal with the change. However, their lack of information gives them a false perception about what the change actually entails. Consequently, employees "slip" into the next phase of **Informed Pessimism**. As employees learn more about the change, reality sets in and grave doubts surface about whether the change can be accomplished. At this point, some employees "check out" of the change (either publicly or privately). The critical stage of any change, however, is the **Valley of Despair**. In this stage, people react with frustration, depression, or anger. These emotions can create a churning or vortex that is hard to escape from without something to break them out. As leaders continue to support employees, communicate about the change, and share successes, people move into **Hopeful Realism**. In this stage, the changes begin to take hold, workers gain a more balanced perspective, and people have hope in realistic solutions to combat specific problems. Finally, as the change momentum builds and personal benefits start to emerge, employees reach the **Informed Optimism** stage. Based on actual experience with the change, employees gain a higher level of optimism and self-confidence.

...

"Getting over a painful experience is much like crossing monkey bars. You have to let go at some point in order to move forward."

—C. S. Lewis, novelist and poet

When managing the Emotional Cycle of Change, it's important to realize three things. First, leaders cannot *force* people through the cycle—people progress at different speeds. Not everyone goes through all of the stages or proceeds through them in a linear fashion. Some stages may be skipped entirely; others may be experienced in a different order; some may be re-experienced again and again if people get stuck in a particular stage for an extended period of time. Leaders can't manipulate the stages. One of our clients declared, "We are not going through the Valley of Despair in this change!" It sounds almost comical, but emotional responses can't be mandated or avoided. However, leaders can help people accelerate through the cycle by managing the change in all the ways we've discussed so far.

Second, leaders must acknowledge that different people are in different stages, and they must align their communication and support accordingly. We know of leaders who tried to avoid the messy, emotional side of change. They didn't acknowledge the emotions associated with the change or help people transition through the cycle. Consequently, their change initiative failed. How can you tell where people are in the emotional cycle? The list below captures common emotions that employees experience in each stage—emotions that you must acknowledge and address to help people transition.

- **Uninformed Optimism**. Primary behavior: denial. When changes first occur, people often feel shock and disbelief. A typical reaction is to hold on to what is familiar from the past in hopes the change will simply go away. In this stage, people may carry on with "business as usual" and seem uninterested in the change. Or they simply may not believe management is really serious about the change.

- **Informed Pessimism**. Primary behavior: fear. Once people are convinced that the change is real, they typically feel fear and resist or reject the change. Their concerns and uncertainty about the future can be expressed in argument, withdrawal, or even distress and illness. In this stage, typical questions include "Why me? It's not fair!"; "How can this happen to me?"; and "Who is to blame?"

- **Valley of Despair**. Primary behavior: depression. During this stage, people may become silent and spend a lot of time crying and grieving. It's not recommended to attempt to cheer up an individual who is in this stage. Grief is an important emotion that must be processed for people to be able to move on. In this stage, typical statements include "I'm so sad, why bother with anything?"; "It is all going to change soon, so what's the point?"; and "Why go on?"

- **Hopeful Realism**: Primary behavior: hope. Once people begin to accept the change and have ownership in it, they begin to feel hope and enthusiasm for the future. In this stage, people often demonstrate their acceptance of the change by starting lots of new initiatives. Typical statements are "I think it's going to work"; and "Shouldn't we be seeing results by now?"

- **Informed Optimism**: Primary behavior: acceptance. In this last stage, people come to terms with the change. The energy generated in the **Hopeful Realism** stage slowly builds a sense of commitment to the change and an understanding of the time and effort required to implement it effectively. Employees start working together in a consistent, unfrenzied, and focused way that produces results. Statements emerge like "It's going to be okay."

...

"I'm not afraid of death. It's just that I don't
want to be there when it happens."

—Woody Allen, American filmmaker

Can you see these different emotions in your people? As you get better at recognizing the stages, you can plan appropriate support and communication to help people make their own personal transitions more quickly. Effective transition management supports employees so they can make the emotional commitment to do something in a new way.

To help change leaders or sponsors identify where people are in the emotional cycle, we use the following simple activity designed for teams.

Directions: Create a wall chart with the Emotional Cycle of Change. Gather pens and sticky notes. Assemble your team.

Part A: Leaders. Think about your change initiative and answer the following questions:

1. Which emotional stage are you in?
2. What do you need to do to move to the next stage? What's getting in your way of making the transition? What do you need?
3. What needs to happen for you to lead more effectively?
4. What will you do starting tomorrow?

Part B: Team. Think about your own reaction to the change and answer the following questions:

1. Where are you in the Emotional Cycle of Change? Be prepared to place a blank sticky note on the wall chart to acknowledge your current emotional reaction.
2. What do you need to transition to the next stage? Capture one to two ideas on a sticky note and be prepared to place it on the wall chart.

Part C: Discussion. Standing exercise at the wall chart.

1. Ask team members to place their sticky notes on the wall chart—both the blank one that represents where they are in the stages and the one with ideas to help them transition.
2. Acknowledge that everyone is in a different stage, and that's normal.
3. Ask them to share the things that will help them transition to the next stage.

We know of teams that have done this simple activity at the beginning of their team meeting every six weeks. The data it produces is a great resource for leaders to use as they shape their communication and change efforts around the things that will help people make the transitions.

The third thing a change leader or sponsor can do to manage the Emotional Cycle of Change is to accelerate the transition process and make the Valley of Despair shallower. The table below lists generic head, hands, and heart actions you can take to help people move through the cycle more quickly.

Leadership Actions to Enable Transition

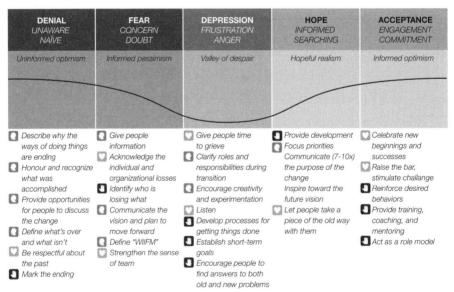

DENIAL	FEAR	DEPRESSION	HOPE	ACCEPTANCE
UNAWARE	CONCERN	FRUSTRATION	INFORMED	ENGAGEMENT
NAÏVE	DOUBT	ANGER	SEARCHING	COMMITMENT
Uninformed optimism	Informed pessimism	Valley of despair	Hopeful realism	Informed optimism
Describe why the ways of doing things are ending	Give people information	Give people time to grieve	Provide development	Celebrate new beginnings and successes
Honour and recognize what was accomplished	Acknowledge the individual and organizational losses	Clarify roles and responsibilities during transition	Focus priorities Communicate (7-10x) the purpose of the change	Raise the bar, stimulate challange
Provide opportunities for people to discuss the change	Identify who is losing what	Encourage creativity and experimentation	Inspire toward the future vision	Reinforce desired behaviors
Define what's over and what isn't	Communicate the vision and plan to move forward	Listen	Let people take a piece of the old way with them	Provide training, coaching, and mentoring
Be respectful about the past	Define "WIIFM"	Develop processes for getting things done		Act as a role model
Mark the ending	Strengthen the sense of team	Establish short-term goals		
		Encourage people to find answers to both old and new problems		

Obviously, the transition ideas employees shared in the team activity are specific to them and should be your primary focus before these generic ideas. The Head, Hands, Heart tool also reveals additional actions you can take to make the transition shorter for your people.

The bottom line is that you must acknowledge and address the psychological process employees go through to make a change. This internal change depends on letting go of what has been comfortable and familiar and accepting the new reality required in the future. If you fail to support employees' emotional transitions, then you should expect nothing more than failure to change the organization.

Factor 3: Enabling Greater Engagement

In a key study about organizational change, the global management-consulting firm Bain & Company reported that 65% of initiatives required significant behavioral change on the part of frontline employees—something that managers often fail to consider or plan for in advance.[7] Helping employees understand and make those significant behavioral changes is what enabling greater engagement is all about.

...

"The role of a creative leader is not to have all the ideas;
it's to *create* a culture where everyone can have ideas
and feel that they're valued."

—Sir Ken Robinson, English author, speaker, and
international advisor on education in the arts

Our colleague Dave Jennings explains to clients that a leader's role is to climb the figurative change mountain, look around to determine the direction, come back down the mountain and engage others, and then take everyone back up the mountain. Yet most leaders summit the mountain and get so enraptured with the view they forget to go back down to get the rest of the organization. How do we know? Research shows that only 25% of employees are highly engaged. And despite all that organizations have done to increase engagement over the last ten years, the numbers haven't changed significantly around the world. The needle is stuck! No wonder change is hard—we are relying on one out of every four people in the organization to go the extra mile to implement the change. What about everyone else? They fall into three categories: (1) moderately engaged (30%), (2) disengaged (25%), and (3) highly disengaged (20%).[8]

In our experience, workforce engagement closely parallels change engagement in the beginning of change. Employees will typically approach change with the same level of energy and motivation as their regular work. The good news is that 55% of the workforce is either highly or somewhat engaged to tackle your change initiative. The bad news is that 45% of employees are either somewhat or highly disengaged. Enabling engagement means moving the needle by getting that 45% to own the change, while also enabling the highly engaged to stay energized and motivated through the change process as new roles, work, and direction are clarified.

Jack Welch, former CEO of General Electric, said, "There are only three measurements that tell you nearly everything you need to know about your organization's overall performance: employee engagement, customer satisfaction, and cash flow. It goes without saying that no company, small or large, can win over the long run without energized employees who believe in the mission and understand how to achieve it."[9] We were surprised when we read this quote. For years, Jack was about cash flow, profitability, and dominating a market sector. So why did he list employee engagement as the first measure of overall performance? Look at the research about why engagement is critical:

- **Operating Income**: Companies with high employee engagement have a 19% increase in operating income and a 28% growth in earnings per share.[10]

- **Shareholder Returns:** A group of companies with higher levels of engagement generated annual shareholder returns that were 9.3 percentage points higher than the return for the S&P 500 index.[11]

- **Total Shareholder Return:** High-engagement firms have 19% higher total shareholder return than the average. In low-engagement organizations, total shareholder return was actually 44% below average.[12]

- **Business Results:** Business units scoring in the top quartile of employee engagement, compared with those in the bottom quartile, enjoyed on average[13]

  ○ 12% higher customer satisfaction,
  ○ 16% higher profitability,
  ○ 18% greater productivity,
  ○ 49% lower employee turnover,
  ○ 49% fewer safety incidents,
  ○ 37% lower absenteeism, and
  ○ 60% fewer quality defects.

- **Sales:** Electronics retailer Best Buy reports that stores that increase employee engagement by a 10th of a point (on a five-point scale) will see a $100,000 increase in sales for the year.[14]

- **Customer Satisfaction:** A Manpower survey of call center customers and employees reported that centers with high employee satisfaction also have high customer satisfaction. Alternatively, centers with low employee satisfaction have low customer satisfaction.[15]

These are the kinds of results business leaders are looking for. In fact, these results are often the reason for a change initiative in the first place! But results won't come without engagement in change.

In the book *The Employee Engagement Mindset,* which Kendall co-authored with Tim Clark and other colleagues, *engagement* is defined as follows:

- A measure of passion, commitment, attachment, and contribution to the change

- The connection to the change and to the organization

- The comprehensive expression of motivation and desire to contribute

- The extent to which employees get results with energy, passion, and purpose; engage with customers/stakeholders better, innovate faster, and execute more reliably; and demonstrate focus, motivation, and commitment

When leaders attain this level of engagement, they have created a lethal, competitive weapon for themselves in whatever endeavor they choose to undertake.

...

"Work is about a search for daily meaning as well as daily bread, for recognition as well as cash, for astonishment rather than torpor; in short, for a sort of life, rather than a Monday-to-Friday sort of dying."

—Louis "Studs" Terkel, American author, actor, broadcaster, and Pulitzer Prize winner

So What's the Problem?

Let's take another look at the statistics. You can plan on 55% of your workforce being highly or somewhat engaged to tackle your change initiative. The real problem lies in the 45% who are flat out disengaged.

For change to be successful, your people need to have passion, commitment, and motivation—but slightly less than half aren't there. The **somewhat disengaged** are those who have disconnected rationally, emotionally, and motivationally. They are employees who have essentially "checked out," sleepwalk through their workday, or put time—but not passion—into their work. The **highly disengaged** are employees who actively campaign against the change in various ways. They may try to undermine what their engaged coworkers are trying to accomplish. Even the **somewhat or moderately engaged** employees pose a bit of a challenge. While they may support the change, they aren't performing at their full capability, chiefly because they don't have the kind of rational, emotional, and motivational connections that drive discretionary effort.

Your change project is at risk with these kinds of engagement levels. But the highly engaged employees think and behave differently. They take primary responsibility for their careers, their success, and their fulfillment. They own their own engagement. They don't wait for the organization to engage them. They proactively engage in change themselves.

...

"This is the true joy in life—being used for a purpose recognized by yourself as a mighty one; being thoroughly worn out before you are thrown on the scrap heap; being a force of nature instead of a feverish, selfish little clod of ailments and grievances complaining that the world will not devote itself to making you happy."

—George Bernard Shaw, playwright, essayist, and novelist

What Can You Do about It?

Research shows that organizational conditions can enable engagement—to a point. (Think of all the research from the "Great Place to

Work" surveys published by *Fortune* every year.) But the real power of engagement comes from the balanced combination of organizational conditions and individual drivers.

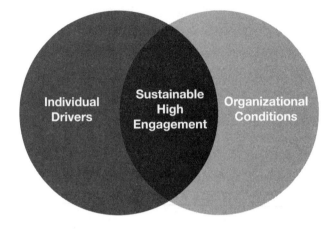

High Engagement = Individual Drivers + Organizational Conditions

Notice that we said "balanced" combination. If there is too much or too little focus on either side of the equation, the highest levels of engagement won't occur. Organizations (outside-in) are responsible for enabling conditions; individuals (inside-out) are responsible for individual behavior. If both elements come together, the results are highly engaged individuals, teams, and organizations that get extraordinary business results. As a change leader, you need to (1) tap into those who are highly engaged and (2) create conditions that will engage the rest. If you don't actively address the issue of engagement, you are betting your change effort on employee goodwill and chance. What would be the odds of success in that case? Almost none.

John Wesley, the founder of Methodism, once remarked, "I light myself on fire, and people come to see me burn." But that actually didn't turn out to be true. They didn't simply watch Wesley "burn" for some sort of entertainment and then go back to business as usual.

Wesley's passion was such an inspiration that thousands of people left the Church of England—a profound and risky personal change—to become followers. Today, eighty million adherents worldwide prove that Wesley's fire and passion engaged and changed the hearts and minds of many.

Your change isn't really that different from his. So how do you figuratively "light yourself on fire" and then inspire that same passion in others? Take a look at the six drivers of individual engagement below.

Six Drivers to Engage People		
Connecting Plug into power sources	**Shaping** Make it your own	**Learning** Learn at the speed of change
Stretching Go to the outer limits	**Achieving** Jump into the cycle	**Contributing** Get beyond self

Connecting

Plug into Power Sources. This driver is about helping people create connections with the change initiative. Connections are created in four ways: (1) Socially: the relationships created and deepened by the change among coworkers and teams; (2) Intellectually: the intellectual challenge of the change work; (3) Environmentally/Culturally: the environmental or cultural modifications as a result of the change; and (4) Inspirationally: the connection to the cause, the purpose, or the goal of the change initiative. Here are some of the questions you might ask to engage people using this driver:

- What new social connections and relationships need to be established within and between teams?

- How can we involve those affected by the change in solving difficult problems?

- What intellectual challenges arise because of the change that might engage people?

- What can we do to inspire people to the cause, mission, vision, values, or goals of the change?

- How can we connect people's individual passions with the organization's new direction?

...

"We don't accomplish anything in this world alone . . .
and whatever happens is the result of the whole tapestry
of one's life and all the weavings of individual threads
from one to another that creates something."

—Sandra Day O'Connor, former US Supreme Court justice

Shaping

Make It Your Own. Shaping allows employees to customize, personalize, and tailor their work and work life within certain parameters. Employees are empowered to influence their work conditions—what they do, when they do it, and with whom they do it—which creates ownership. In short, this driver allows people to customize their professional life to meet their preferences. It doesn't mean that when things are changing people get a blank sheet of paper to redefine their jobs any way they choose. Of course, there are real limits. But the idea is to give people as much control as possible to define their work and take advantage of new opportunities. Here are some of the questions you might ask to engage people using this driver:

- How can we link the goals and intended outcomes of the change with the individual goals of employees?

- What might get in the way of employees accomplishing their personal goals? How can we remove those roadblocks?

- Which work environment variables can we shape to create a more engaging experience (e.g., work schedules, work location, work teams, work processes)?

- What extrinsic rewards would help achieve the goals of the change?

...

"In the long run, we shape our lives and we shape ourselves. The process never ends until we die. And the choices we make are ultimately our own responsibility."

—Eleanor Roosevelt, longest-serving first lady of the United States

Learning

Learn at the Speed of Change. Learning is the process of acquiring knowledge, skills, and experience. The fear of being unqualified or not having the right skills can paralyze some people. Consequently, this driver is about helping people learn what they need to implement the change successfully. Here are some of the questions you might ask to engage people using this driver:

- How prepared are employees to step into this new change? What are they missing? How can we help close the gap?

- What new knowledge, skills, and experience do employees need to be successful in this change? How will people gain them?

- What coaching do people need? How can they coach each other?

- How can we solicit, understand, and implement feedback throughout the change process?

...

"Live as if you were to die tomorrow. Learn as if
you were to live forever."

—Mahatma Gandhi, leader of Indian nationalism

Stretching

Go to the Outer Limits. Stretching is the process of getting people out of their comfort zone, passing through the discomfort zone, and pushing to the outer limits. Isn't that one definition of change? Stretching increases people's capacity to perform—and that's when engagement goes to much higher levels. Even though the stretch can create some discomfort, and even some pain, it's also when people feel the most exhilarated. Here are some questions for this driver:

- How will this change be a stretch for employees? What will be uncomfortable for people?

- How can we help employees interpret and manage the risk?

- What obstacles might get in the way of people stretching? How can we remove those obstacles?

- How can we tie the stretch to implement the change with employees' personal development goals?

...

"Only in growth, reform, and change, paradoxically enough,
is true security to be found."

—Anne Morrow Lindbergh, American writer

Achieving

Jump into the Cycle. Achieving is the process of focusing and sustaining people's efforts to accomplish something meaningful. If people are unwilling to stretch and develop in the first place, chances are they won't achieve much. But once they begin to accomplish consequential work, then achievement creates its own rewards—intrinsic rewards that cause people to say, "Hey, I want to do more." Research shows that every time people accomplish something, even if it's small, it replenishes their energy, boosts confidence, deepens fulfillment, and gives them the motivation to keep trying. These short-term wins can accelerate the change process. Here are some questions to increase engagement through this driver:

- How can we treat people with respect and dignity during the change?

- Are people overloaded with minutiae or busywork? What can we do to eliminate this type of work so they can focus on the change?

- What small wins should we aim for to fuel the achievement cycle?

...

"It is hard to fail, but it is worse never to have tried to succeed."

—Theodore Roosevelt, former US president

Contributing

Get Beyond Self. One definition of contribution is "effort directed beyond self toward a meaningful purpose." Human beings want to make a difference—it's an innate need. During exit interviews when employees are asked, "What is it that you value the most from the experience you have had in this organization?" thousands of them have responded with (1) their relationships and (2) their personal contributions. Engagement goes up when people can contribute to something with higher meaning and purpose. Here are some questions for this driver:

- How can we encourage and reward people to take risks and challenge the status quo?

- What is the bigger contribution we are asking people to make? What is the meaningful purpose behind the change?

- Have we clarified the requirements, results, and measures of people's jobs?

- What bureaucracy can we eliminate so people can focus on adding real value?

...

"It is one of the most beautiful compensations in life that no man can sincerely try to help another without helping himself."

—Ralph Waldo Emerson, essayist, lecturer, and poet

SUMMARY

Louis Gerstner said of his experience in leading the turnaround at IBM, "The best leaders are change agents, constantly driving their institutions to adapt and advance faster than their competitors do."[16] The constant churn of change Gerstner is talking about demands all-hands engagement. It's dealing with people's emotions and issues—overcoming natural resistance to the change, supporting people as they transition through the Emotional Cycle of Change, and eventually igniting their fire and passion toward the change work. Sometimes accelerating engagement feels too esoteric or obscure. It's easier to deal with the nuts and bolts of the change—process modifications, policy updates, detailed presentations, Gantt charts—than to patiently work with someone through the Valley of Despair. But ignoring the intimate work of engagement dooms the change to failure. Remember, things don't change until people do. So change must be personal. It must be intimate and emotional. Change leaders must be prepared to convince the heads, hold the hands, and change the hearts of their employees as they strive toward a new and brighter future.

CHAPTER SUMMARY

KEY POINTS

- Engaging people in the change process is the most difficult, time-consuming, overlooked, and greatest opportunity left unaddressed by leaders of change. If the difficult issues you face are anything like those in most organizations, simple and quick-fix solutions aren't going to create sustainable change.

- Resistance is a natural reaction to any change and the biggest challenge to successful implementation. Simply announcing what the changes will be and expecting everyone to comply is not enough. Change leaders must work through and neutralize the natural resistance to change by providing information and support to help employees successfully navigate transitions.

- Understanding the Commitment Curve, and assessing where employees are on the curve, helps leaders anticipate the level of resistance to change and plan ways to overcome it. Effective leaders will work to engage the Heads, Hands, and Hearts of people to accelerate the pace at which they arrive at the Commitment Phase.

- The golden rule of change is "Don't do to them what you wouldn't want done to you." Stakeholder Analysis and Engagement, Communication Planning and Events, and Involvement Strategies are three tools that will help leaders to lead change like they would want to be led.

- Leaders must acknowledge and address the psychological process employees go through to make a change. Managing the emotional cycle of change enables employees to mourn, mend, and ultimately transition to the new state of things.

- When managing the Emotional Cycle of Change, it's important to realize three things. First, leaders cannot *force* people through the cycle—people progress at different speeds. Second, leaders must acknowledge that different people are in different stages, and they must align their communication and change support accordingly. And third, as a change leader or sponsor, you have the ability to accelerate the transition process so that people move through the cycle more quickly.

- Workforce engagement closely parallels change engagement. Employees will typically approach change with the same level of energy and motivation as their regular work. Enabling engagement means getting the disengaged to own the change while also enabling the highly engaged to stay energized and motivated through the change process as new roles, work, and direction are clarified.

- The real power of engagement comes from the balanced combination of organizational conditions and individual drivers. As a change leader, you need to tap into those who are highly engaged, and create conditions that will engage the rest. Six drivers that will engage people in change include (1) Connecting, (2) Shaping, (3) Learning, (4) Stretching, (5) Achieving, and (6) Contributing.

5

ACCELERATING LEADERSHIP

"It is a terrible thing to look over your shoulder when you are trying to lead—and find no one there."

—Franklin Delano Roosevelt, former US president

n 1993, a search committee comprised of a few board members and two search firms was looking for the next CEO of one of the biggest companies in America. Not only did this company employ hundreds of thousands of people, but it had become, in some people's minds, a national treasure. Two committee members described the characteristics of the kind of CEO they were looking for. The first member said,

> The committee members and I are totally open-minded about who the next person will be and where he or she will come from. What is critically important is the person must be a proven, effective leader—one who is skilled at generating and [leading] change.[1]

And the second member said, "The challenge for the next leader would begin with driving strategic and cultural change."[2]

On the surface, these two comments don't seem unusual and could apply to many organizations searching for a new CEO. But what if you knew the company in question was IBM? Wouldn't you think the most important attributes would be understanding the computer industry, being an expert in technology, or leading innovative product development? Instead, the board was very clear that it needed someone who could skillfully *generate* and *lead* change.

Interestingly enough, Kendall worked at IBM shortly before the search for the new CEO began. It was a great job right out of school—great company, great experience, and a great resume builder. But it didn't always feel great to work there. One hot day in July, when Kendall was working in the Utah sales and marketing office, he arrived to work wearing a short-sleeved white shirt and tie. Upon entering the large, open area where the marketing and systems specialists sat, Kendall noticed his manager quickly rise from his desk and hurry out of his office toward him. When they were face-to-face, Kendall's manager said, "That's not going to work!" Huh? Kendall had just arrived. What could possibly be wrong already?

After a few back-and-forth exchanges, Kendall realized that his manager was talking about his shirt—it was a short-sleeved white shirt versus the traditional long-sleeved white shirt that was the uniform for male employees. The IBM dress code was so ingrained in the culture that any variation was frowned upon.

One Friday the head of sales arrived at work wearing a light blue shirt. The office buzzed with comments like "What is he doing?" and "Doesn't he know the division manager isn't going to be pleased?" In both cases, Kendall was shocked. He thought, "Really? We're getting creamed in the marketplace and we're worried about wearing the wrong shirt?" The company was so internally focused on silly policies like dress code and who got which office that it was missing or ignoring some of the bigger marketplace trends. For example, at that time the following things were true:[3]

- Sales and profits had declined at an alarming rate creating a tenuous cash position.

- Mainframe revenue (IBM's core product at the time) had dropped from $13 billion in 1990 to less than $7 billion in 1993.

- Prices were much higher than competitors', and the company's image was in tatters.

- The stock price had dropped from a high of $43 a share in 1987 to $12 a share in 1993.

- Some outside experts were giving odds of no better than one in five that IBM could be saved.

In short, the company was slipping rapidly. And the media and business writers alike were having a field day with statements like these:

> There is a serious possibility that IBM is finished as a force in the industry. Bill Gates, the software tycoon whom everybody in the industry loves to hate, denies having said in an unguarded moment that IBM will fold in seven years. But Gates may be right. IBM is now an also-ran in almost every major computer technology introduced since 1980. . . . Traditional big computers are not going to disappear overnight, but they are old technology, and the realm in which they hold sway is steadily shrinking. The brontosaurus moved deeper into the swamps when the mammals took over the forests, but one day it ran out of swamps.[4]

...

The question for the present is whether IBM can survive. From our analysis thus far, it is clear that we think its prospects are very bleak.[5]

...

The world will look very different by the time IBM pulls itself together—assuming it can pull itself together—and IBM will never again hold sway over the computer industry.[6]

...

Given this context, it makes sense that the search committee was looking for a CEO who could transform the organization. They found that trait in Lou Gerstner, who was hired as CEO in April 1993. In the first few months after he joined the firm, Gerstner and Thomas J. Watson Jr., former CEO of IBM and the son of its founder (and seventy-nine years old at the time), had ongoing conversations about changes in the organization. In a somewhat animated and agitated tone, Watson told Gerstner that he needed to shake up the firm "from top to bottom and to take whatever steps were necessary to get it back on track."[7]

Essentially, the board and Watson were encouraging Gerstner to accelerate the speed of change by accelerating his own leadership. And that's exactly what he did. Gerstner went on to not only save the company, but to enable significant growth because he knew how to lead change.

What would the leadership job description look like given the situation you are facing? If you had to be replaced, what attributes would the board be looking for in your successor? Technical and social skills are basic, minimum requirements. But the ability to lead change is unique and in higher demand today. One of the biggest derailers we have seen in good leaders is their inability to lead themselves, their organization, their team, their peers, and even their boss. This leads to a lack of scale and an inability to leverage resources, and it hampers the organization's capacity to grow.

...

"Genius means little more than

the faculty of perceiving in an unhabitual way."

—William James, American psychologist

LEADING WITH YOUR HEAD UP

One of our colleagues, Leslie Sturzenberger, shared a quote with us from the CEO of an automotive firm that she worked with. The CEO said, "I want us to learn to lead with our heads up verses manage with our heads down." For years, IBM had been internally focused, managing its business with its head down. But when leaders learned to lead with their heads up, they accelerated change and found solutions from across the business that solved current and future needs of IBM customers. They changed the customer experience.

Countless books have been written on leadership. Our purpose here is to focus on how to lead in a way that accelerates change by accelerating the individual and collective leadership capacity to transform the business. We've picked a few key aspects of leading change that may be missed by otherwise good leaders.

A study conducted by Development Dimensions International (DDI) revealed that leaders spent 41% of their time managing (planning, doing administrative tasks, scheduling, etc.) and only 25% interacting (conversing with peers, team members, supervisors, and customers). But given a preference, "leaders would nearly double the time they spend interacting and cut in half their time spent managing."[8] Why? Because organizations that value interactions among leaders have twice the leader experience as competitors, three and a half times the leadership bench strength, twice the financial impact, and 20% more leaders ready to fill critical roles—all of which are important to getting change implemented effectively and growing the business. In a *McKinsey Quarterly* article, the authors found that quality interactions have the potential to create durable, competitive advantage, and they refer to this capability as "relationship capital."[9] No wonder leaders would rather spend their time interacting!

...

"Historically there have been only two basic ways to aggregate and amplify human capabilities. They were bureaucracy and markets. Then in the last ten years we have added a third—networks."

—Gary Hamel, author and professor, London Business School

Despite these findings, too often senior leaders rely on technical capability to lead change, and they don't invest in relationship capital. If you don't learn to lead change and foster the necessary relationships, your change initiative will sputter. To use a financial metaphor, if you don't have any capital in the relationship bank accounts of the people who need to support the change, the change initiative will be bankrupt. Peter Drucker said, "Effective leadership is not about making speeches or being liked; leadership is defined by results not attributes." In today's world, leaders can't get results by themselves. They must work with and through other people to make change happen. If they don't, they will discover the reality of Roosevelt's statement— they will look over their shoulder and find they are leading no one.

HOW THIS BECAME REAL FOR US

The importance of strong leadership during change became clear to us many years ago. We were working with a client in the newspaper business. The industry was undergoing major technological transformations, and this particular organization was feeling its own irrelevancy. They needed a major change to get back in the game.

We had been selected from three or four other consulting firms to lead the change transformation of the newspaper and related businesses. Part of the goal was to downsize from a $1 billion operating budget to $300 million in two years while at the same time keeping the business running and solvent. This change seemed monumental for a company that had been stable for fifty-plus years! Having been hired by the general manager and the task group, we did not have a strong relationship with the CEO, Bill (not his real name), but we had been in a few meetings with him during the first week of the project. Several of those sessions had contentious issues, and Tony sensed some resistance to our questions and bold approach, particularly from Bill.

One morning, our team was in the "war room" that we had set up on the executive floor not far from Bill's office. Suddenly, the door swung open with a loud bang, and Bill stood there and looked around the room, finally settling his gaze on Tony. He pointed his finger and said with a loud voice, "You, come with me." We were all a bit shocked, but Tony followed him out to his office suite without a word. Back in the "war room," our team was sure we were being fired from the project. Kendall said, "Pack up all our materials while I check flight schedules." When Tony got to Bill's office, the CEO invited him to sit in the parlor area of his spacious work space and said, "I need your help." Tony was surprised and shocked! Bill went on to say that he was struggling mightily with the changes he needed to make personally to his own leadership skills as well as the extensive changes that needed to be made to the business. He asked if Tony would coach him through the next year of transition. Tony was deeply empathetic and impressed with Bill's transparency. Instead of firing us, he was simply asking for help.

Over the next hour, Bill and Tony discussed the change in some detail. Bill shared the personal difficulty he was having in dismantling the organization that he had built over the past fifteen years. Tony agreed to work with him, and for the next year they met once or twice a week to explore his issues around leading the change. What surprised us most was that Tony and Bill primarily discussed the CEO's feelings and challenges and seldom the actual business changes. It was fascinating to see him grow, and as he evolved and progressed, so did the change effort. We had read a great deal about the power of leadership in change, but we had never experienced it so up close and personal.

Both Bill and the business transformed over the next two years. It rightsized, redefined its product, and expanded its delivery methods. Today, it is thriving once again in the new world of media. This real example epitomized the saying "Organizations don't change, people do," including leaders. Bill's personal transformation led the way for other leaders to grow and change and for the business to change.

Consider a time when you were part of a great team—a team that achieved something important with amazing grace and incredible team spirit. This might have been a sports team, a business project, a church group, or a family reunion. What did it feel like to be a part of that team? What was your role? What were the roles of others? How did you relate to the other team members? What was the nature of leadership on the team? What did the team accomplish? And finally, what is your hypothesis about what made the team so great?

We have asked these questions hundreds of times with different groups, and here are some of the things we commonly hear. Great teams have the following:

- A powerful mission
- A high commitment to that mission
- Great communication among team members
- Strong trust between members
- Balanced leadership

- Clear roles

- Well-defined processes and systems for getting things done

- The right mix of players and skillsets

Virtually everyone says a critical component of a successful team is the "power of leadership." Upon further discussion, employees have said that leadership was not necessarily required to motivate, but rather to set up the team for success and help it achieve and maintain momentum.

...

"Organizations don't outperform their leaders; they reflect them. An organization's ability to adapt and adjust to shifting demands is really a function of a leader's ability to lead change."

—Timothy R. Clark, author and change expert

Now if you think of a great change effort that you've been a part of, you will most likely see the same elements for success. Leaders make the difference in great teams and in change! We have also asked the question "What was the nature of leadership in change?" The responses are remarkably consistent from hundreds of respondents:

- Leaders had high energy, passion for the change, and were very visible in championing the effort.

- Leaders balanced high standards and accountability with a climate of feedback and understanding.

- Leaders trusted and empowered their people to contribute their brilliance to the change.

- Leaders were optimistic, but also transparent and realistic about barriers and obstacles.

- The most successful leaders didn't "boil the ocean!" In other words, they knew change was hard and took time and energy, so they focused on only two or three specific changes at a time.

- They paid the price to build a healthy emotional and intellectual bank account with each critical person in their network. (Emotional intelligence is a hallmark of the best-in-class change leaders who model self-awareness and self-management and who continually "walk the talk" of the change and maintain the integrity of the change process.)

- They made convincing, forceful decisions. They were willing to step out and up to demonstrate to the organization that the status quo was not going to be the way forward.

It would have been easy (and quite common) for Lou Gerstner to mandate change, downsize divisions, and delegate the leadership and accountability of change to others at IBM. Instead, he became the champion for change (as his job description had specified) and engaged in the process as an active leader of change.

The behaviors and actions of a leader are, in our opinion, the most critical element in change. You must be the change you seek in others. Like our client Bill, making the brave and humbling decision to work on your abilities to lead change is one of the most critical decisions you will make. If that makes you feel like the success of change is primarily on your shoulders, that's because it is.

...

"Let him who would move the world first move himself."

—Socrates, Greek philosopher

LEADING, NOT MANAGING CHANGE:
A BETTER PARADIGM FOR SUCCESS

In the summer of 1995, Tony found himself in an office of one of the tallest skyscrapers in New York City. He had been introduced to several partners at McKinsey and Company's New York office via some work with a mutual client. These particular partners were critically examining and studying effective change to support some of their Fortune 100 clients who were going through major transformations.

The firm had a passion for excellence in strategy, but they were confounded and a little rattled by the results of an internal study originally titled "Why Bad Things Happen to Great Strategies." The results of the study made it clear that even with the most elegant strategies and solutions, some of the world's top companies were not seeing the results they expected. In fact, the statistic from the study was that 70% of the great strategies were not adopted and realized. The partners at McKinsey and Company were searching for the disconnect. Because honestly, if the world's best companies couldn't make change happen with best-in-class solutions, then who could? We believe the answer lies in the difference between managing change and leading change. Let us explain further.

MANAGING CHANGE

The typical mindset and approach to change we encounter is what we call a "management approach." The management approach usually plays out in this way.[10] A leader sees either an opportunity (e.g., discontinuity in the marketplace) or a gap (e.g., poor results due to outdated systems and processes). The leader assembles an ad hoc team to analyze the situation and establish goals, such as revenue or profitability improvement or some sort of efficiency or customer service measure to close the gap. Upon outlining the change goal, leaders typically identify actions, programs, new roles, and/or organization shifts that will theoretically propel the business to close the gap and achieve the goal. These driving forces are well-intended, no doubt, but more often than not are ill-conceived and too weak to penetrate the real cause of the problem in the first place—the restraining forces that are part of the culture of the organization.

...

"Management is how well it runs when you are there; leadership is how well it runs when you are not."

—Chase LeBlanc, author

A Management Approach

These actions, behaviors, programs, and organizational changes (e.g., restructuring) must be focused and powerful enough to overcome the cultural resistance in the organization until a new norm is established. As we discussed in an earlier chapter, culture is a superpower element that cannot be underestimated. With the management approach to change, leaders often see short-term spikes of success when implementing change only to realize long-term failure because of cultural resistance. Hence the saying "culture eats strategy for breakfast." The result is that the system goes back to where it was, there is a deeper lack of trust and engagement, and the sense of misalignment is as pervasive as ever. Platitudes, pep rallies, training, or threats cannot change this situation. The driving forces that were designed and implemented with the expectation that they would resolve the issues, close the gaps, and improve performance just aren't enough.

The previous illustration aptly depicts the management approach. Leaders push hard on the driving forces. The restraining forces are like springs that coil up and store energy. Over time, these coils rebound and repel the driving forces and the status quo returns. The restraining springs typically come in four forms: (1) a lack of trust, (2) a lack of focus, (3) a lack of engagement, and (4) organizational misalignments. Until these four areas are fully addressed, they continue to push against and repel the drivers. The "as is" culture once again wins the organizational change battle! No wonder leaders feel frustrated when employees go back to doing things the old way.

...

**"The moment there is suspicion about a person's motives,
everything he does becomes tainted."**

—Mahatma Gandhi, leader of Indian nationalism

LEADING CHANGE

A more effective approach than managing change is leading change. This approach plays out similarly, yet it has some key differences. First, a leader identifies a gap or opportunity. Again the gap or opportunity can be around financials, customer service, operational efficiency, safety, sales, etc. From this point of inception, the two approaches diverge in some important ways. The leader assembles an ad hoc team to gather data and involve as many people as possible. For example, we have designed and led "future search" conferences where hundreds of employees gather to capture and expand on the vision and gap, to make it their own, and to contribute to the richness and texture of the vision and outcome. Meanwhile, the leader stays intimately involved with the team and in the process. The product of the analysis is a shared vision of the outcome, the journey, the realized impact, and the gain—in essence, the story of the change. And the leader helps others to understand, accept, and commit to that end state.

By involving employees in the analysis, and helping them understand and commit to the change, the leading approach is significantly more impactful in creating champions of change than the managing approach. Employees are brought on board, engaged in the opportunity, and applauded for their input.

Next, the vision is translated into key measures of success and outcomes not only for the business, but also for employees in a way that engages their head, hands, and heart. (Remember the Head, Hands, and Heart tool we introduced in chapter 4?) You may recall the story of Randy from chapter 2, the Chief Technical Officer at a multibillion-dollar utility who asked the critical question of the CEO, "What exactly do you want me to do differently?" That story has application here as well. Instead of taking offense at Randy's question, the CEO used it as a catalyst to refine his own leadership around the change. He worked hard to create a picture of the vision that ended up changing the heads, hands, and hearts of his people.

That utility achieved #1 in the J.D. Power rankings of utilities for customer service in the nation for three years. It's a perfect example of how leadership acts as the multiplier to remove dissatisfaction, create vision, and guide the practical first steps to overcome the natural resistance found in the culture.

Once the vision and goals are in place, then the heavy lifting begins. In the managing change approach, the paradigm of the leader is to make easy moves that apply outside-in drivers to the system to compel change. In the leading change approach, the leader seeks to understand and eliminate the four underlying barriers—the restraining coils—in the system that prevent the organization from changing (outside-in *and* inside-out barriers). These barriers include mistrust, lack of clarity, low engagement, and organizational misalignments.

Next, effective leaders understand and assess the readiness of the culture to change. Too often leaders think they have it all figured out after a few focus groups or surveys that highlight some of the problems. And consequently these types of leaders try to "turn a switch" hoping things will change. An effective leader of change slows the process down at this point to engage, listen to, understand, adjust, and incorporate the ideas of employees who have much more of a stake in the change than senior leaders. What does that look like? One way is to create an opportunity for employees to come together to dialogue with each other in a safe environment. This type of change forum gives hundreds of people an opportunity to be involved in the change, poke holes in it, and suggest improvements to the approach. Having an environment where employees feel safe and empowered to really contribute honest feedback is the key to success at this stage of the process. Change forums require strong leaders with thick skins, so to speak. It can be hard for leaders to hear what's not working, how the culture isn't everything it's hyped up to be, and to take some heat for bad programs and policies they implemented. This "mining for conflict" can feel a bit like asking a dentist to drill out the cavity without numbing the nerve of the tooth, but it's a critical step to eliminate the restraining forces of mistrust and lack of engagement.

...

**"Many are stubborn in pursuit of the path
they have chosen, few in pursuit of the goal."**

–Friedrich Nietzsche, German philosopher

Finally, the organization is unleashed to begin realigning to the new goals and roles. The leader stays involved and engaged with measuring, reporting, and holding people accountable for progress as the change moves forward. They work hard to remove the restraining forces that often spring up again during implementation.

In summary, managers ask other people to figure it out while leaders work with others to figure it out. Managers are only mildly involved. Leaders are intimately involved. Managers rubber-stamp the goals. Leaders work hard to make sure the goals are right and shared. Managers want a quick fix. Leaders know it will likely take time. Managers push on drivers, such as layoffs and pay cuts. Leaders remove restraining barriers.

If you're a champion of the leading change approach like we are, then consider working on removing the following four restraining barriers to help your change move forward.

...

**"If you are not prepared to lead in the midst of turbulence,
the global age will pin you against the limits of your
ability to respond. If you can't perform on the
new leadership stage, you eventually will fail upward."**

–Timothy R. Clark, author and change expert

Barrier 1: Lack of Trust in Leaders

Lack of trust is the most pervasive and challenging of all the barriers to change. Our colleague Stephen M. R. Covey said that with trust, the tallest of mountains can be ascended. But without trust, even the smallest of issues become like Mount Everest. Covey teaches that trust is the combination of character and competence. You build trust when you deliver on your word, treat others with respect, and are honest and transparent. In the course of many business interactions, with deadlines, power struggles, company politics, and crises, it's common for trust to erode in key relationships.

But you don't have to bankrupt the trust account. Relationships can survive the normal withdrawals that happen in business when leaders make consistent deposits, such as listening, giving recognition to others, and supporting and coaching others along the way. In change, the need for trust deposits is multiplied exponentially! Leaders must ask, engage, listen, respond, and ask again and again to build and rebuild trust, even when discussions are heated or emotional. As one of our colleagues would say during difficult times and discussions, "Great! You see it differently." That spirit creates the relationships of trust that help to overcome the resistance to change. A great leader models this spirit and inspires others to do the same.

...

"Power is actualized only when word and deed have not parted company."

—Hannah Arendt, German political theorist

Barrier 2: Lack of Focus

A lack of clarity is often described by employees as being "in the dark," not knowing what to do differently or how to do it, not knowing what to stop doing, and not understanding what success looks like or how they will be measured. What can a leader do to remove this barrier and ensure clarity? In chapter 2, we discussed how to accelerate focus in change and briefly reviewed the following tools:

- Business Case for Change

- Change Charter

- FROM → TO Behavior Descriptions

- Change Measures

- Change Strategy

Great leaders provide clarity by utilizing these tools and then consistently, even obsessively, following up with progress, measurement, and accountability. These front-end tools create the clarity and then are used on the back end to see if the change is actually happening. Leaders can't disengage from this process at any time. They must be there, running alongside their people, so to speak, and reminding them of what this change is all about and why it's worth it.

...

"Follow through on what you say you're going to do. Your credibility can only be built over time, and it is built from the history of your words and actions."

—Maria Razumich-zec, regional vice president, Hong Kong and Shanghai Hotels

Barrier 3: Lack of Engagement

Engagement is about activating the head, hands, and heart of people in the organization to change. In chapter 4, we reviewed three important components of engagement:

1. Overcoming resistance

2. Managing transitions

3. Enabling greater engagement

Great leaders take an inside-out approach and work on their own engagement first. They can't simply dictate change to others. They must show they are committed to and passionate about the change. Then they move to outside-in and inspire engagement in others. Remember, engagement is the emotional side of change. Leaders empathize with and support employees as they move along the Commitment Curve. They bravely wrestle with the feelings and emotions that could prevent success. At a minimum, leaders ask the following questions of employees as often as necessary until people finally get it:

- Do you know what we are expecting of you in this change?

- Do you know why we are changing?

- Do you know how we will measure the impact of the change?

- Do you have the resources you need to deliver this change? Do you feel supported?

- How can we hold you and others accountable for the change?

- How would you like to be involved in the process of change?

...

"Never doubt that a small group of thoughtful, committed citizens can change the world. Indeed, it is the only thing that ever has."

—Margaret Mead, cultural anthropologist

Barrier 4: Organizational Misalignment

Misalignment is a common condition during change. Getting all of the processes and systems in sync with the change takes time and careful attention. In chapter 3, we outlined how to create alignment from the inside-out and outside-in at the individual, team, and organizational levels. Several years ago, one of our clients in Los Angeles was dealing with a major change to its sales organization. All one hundred of the key people impacted by the change were in the room while the CEO was presenting the change and asking for input. People were asking some questions and giving input. The meeting ended, and everyone rushed out on their way to the airport. We were stuffed in the back of a large elevator with a lot of people. The group in the front of the elevator began listing all of the reasons why the change would not work, most of which had not been mentioned in the session. Clearly the meeting had not created alignment among these one hundred top leaders. So of course, those leaders weren't going to do the necessary work on the processes and systems either. We have since termed this "elevator talk," referring to what happens when leaders of change don't address the most important issues needed for real alignment.

Change leaders can't assume that the memo or meeting is going to get the job done. They work tirelessly with individuals and teams to align the work, roles, processes, and systems with the change. It's the technical "nuts and bolts" side of change that makes employees feel like the system is working with them on the change, not against them.

...

"Leaders spend nowhere near enough time trying to align their organizations with the values and visions already in place."

—Jim Collins, American business consultant, author, and lecturer

After years of trial and error, we believe that leading change (rather than managing it) is truly an accelerator to transformation and change. Addressing barriers takes time and is sometimes uncomfortable. Skillful leaders listen, solve problems, deal with conflict, and relentlessly continue the change conversation. They work on the processes and systems that help people know they mean business—incentives, performance management, training, and compensation. They never pass the ownership to someone else. They never disengage from the process until the change is successfully implemented. That's how they break through barriers and create a group of committed employees willing to enable change. When the leading change approach has been used, we've seen dramatic and transformational results in organizations and teams of all shapes and sizes.

THE LEADERSHIP SPINE

The human body is a great metaphor for change. All of the major systems of the body have unique intelligence and the ability to operate independently and as part of the overall system. Like the body, a change effort has systems, elements, and parts that must work together for the change to be successful. The head, hands, and heart are the employees. The circulatory system is the trust that flows through the whole organization providing needed oxygen and taking away waste. The nervous system is the stream of communication that provides the information needed to function. And the spine is leadership—it's the backbone of the system that provides structure and support for the body to stand and be strong. Let's discuss this idea of the leadership spine in more detail.

Many years ago, we led a change effort as consultants at an American banking institution. The organization was attempting to change its culture from transaction-based to relationship-based, where customer service would be tantamount. We felt like all of the pieces were falling into place well. The top leaders were totally sold on the idea and making it a number one priority; new training programs on customer service were being implemented; and the bank's systems and processes were revamped to be more user friendly. Even the metrics used to score a local bank on its success were aligned with the change. With all of these elements in place, the key was turned to execute the change.

To our surprise, not much happened. Despite all of the work and effort, the status quo pretty much remained the status quo. What was going on? We started reaching out to people for answers. We called various branches to ask why they weren't making the changes they would soon be measured against. It didn't take too many conversations to figure out the problem. We had failed to fully engage the leadership spine. The branch managers and regional managers were *supportive* of the change, but they were not real *champions* of the change. This important group of leaders was the last to know, the last to be consulted, and the last to be trained in the entire effort. They felt a bit overlooked in the overall process. The steering committee had pushed on to implementation without engaging the spine of the business. Consequently, the frontline employees didn't receive the proper messages or support from their immediate managers and supervisors in the local branches.

Steve Dichter, a McKinsey partner and contributor to the book *Real Change Leaders*, once told us that the most pivotal role in a change effort is the local manager, because managers are the ones who have a real allegiance to and relationship with frontline workers. Many employees join firms because of the brand, work environment, and type of work. However, they stay because of the relationship of trust they have with their immediate supervisor. During our change effort with the bank, we made the classic mistake of not fully engaging this most critical element of the leadership spine—the mid-level manager.

We first came across the notion of the leadership spine from working and studying with Daryl Conner, founder and CEO of Conner

Partners. Daryl often says that the "change effort is only as strong as the spine or link of key leaders supporting it." There is a huge difference between a leader who supports change and one who champions the change. Remember the Battle of Trafalgar described in chapter 2? Imagine that you were in the "war room" of the British fleet before the battle and think about what might have transpired. Perhaps three things happened:

1. The case for change and needed outcome were clearly established. The situation was dire, and the alternatives were few.

2. The ship captains became champions of the change. They knew that success or failure hinged on them.

3. A spine of committed leaders was created that was so strong that the bond of trust carried them to a historic victory even when their leader was lost.

Imagine the strength of the spine going further down the chain of command from the captains to the crew leaders to the shipmates. Imagine the level of communication needed between captains and ships during the battle!

Truly engaging and empowering the leadership spine starting with the CEO and moving down to directors, managers, and supervisors accelerates change and ups your odds of success. What percentage of your team leaders are so committed to success that they would push forward in the most challenging and dangerous of situations? Put yourself in a "war room" situation where you are the general attempting to empower your people to take on real leadership in a change effort. What could you say or do that would inspire your captains to bond together, fight to overcome difficult obstacles, and give their best effort even in your absence? This is the essence of what we are describing as a strong leadership spine.

...

"When spiderwebs unite, they can tie up a lion."

—Ethiopian proverb

Let us share with you an exercise we use with clients to help them determine the strength of their change leadership. Draw a spine (i.e., a thick line with small horizontal lines running through it). Starting at the top of the spine, write down the leadership chain of command— the VPs, directors, managers, supervisors, and key teams—involved in your change. Running down the right side, rank each person's commitment level to the change from 1–5, where 5 = high commitment and 1 = no commitment. Running down the left side, categorize each person's level of capability to get the change done using red, yellow, and green, where red = not capable, yellow = needs some help, and green = fully capable.

Now look at the results of your work and answer the following questions:

- What would have to happen to raise the commitment or capability scores of your key leaders?

- What can you do to support each of them?

- What can they do for/with each other?

- What can the organization do to more fully activate the leadership spine?

While the spine for a human body is a critical structural and neural housing mechanism, in today's complex organizations, going vertical is not enough! To accelerate change, you must also branch out horizontally, which means establishing the critical interfaces across the business that need to collaborate with each other to ensure success.

We were recently involved with a Fortune 50 company that was experiencing a major discontinuity in its sales space because of the rise of virtual retail. Business as usual was no longer possible. The silo-oriented approach to success that drove the business in the past would not work. The vice presidents of major parts of the organization were forced to work collaboratively in planning, designing, and executing the business strategy. The leaders of the major functions and lines of business (who once made all their own decisions) suddenly had to collaborate with each other. It was a major cultural shift, and people didn't have the knowledge, skills, or motivation to work horizontally.

Senior leaders soon noticed that changes were not taking hold, and the business started losing ground to virtual competition. A vocal minority promoted a return to the status quo to wait out the disruption, but executives knew that "business as usual" was no safe haven. They tried another approach to engage the leadership spine. They split the top leaders of the business into two camps—one camp of operators of the business and another camp of change innovators. Their intention was to force greater collaboration and change. Ultimately, this experiment was ineffective as the strategies and changes created by the camp of change innovators were not well received by the operators. Once again, the business stalled and two years later it was reorganized. But the new organizational structure still didn't solve the collaboration issue. We were hired at this point, and we listened as the saga of the past several years was retold. We decided to try something different. We set up numerous offsite sessions with the top leaders to clarify the change strategy, teach and learn a new operating system, and most importantly, build relationships horizontally so people would feel comfortable working with each other. These sessions created a leadership spine of champions critical for success moving forward. After years of struggle, the business finally started moving in the right direction as the silos began breaking down. This project was a powerful reminder to us, yet again, of the need for a strong spine of leaders, both vertically and horizontally, who are committed to the change vision and supportive of each other.

...

"Everyone thinks of changing the world,

but no one thinks of changing himself."

—Leo Tolstoy, Russian novelist

THE LEADER'S SHADOW

We have discovered one other critical element to accelerating change through leadership. We call it the leader's shadow.

The leader's shadow is the overall integrity and quality of a leader portrayed in how they lead change in several key areas:

- What he/she says

- How he/she acts

- What he/she measures

- How he/she prioritizes

- How he/she develops self and others

The first key area—what a leader says—is the least impactful. Actions, measurements, and priorities are better gauges of a leader's true commitment to change. Employees naturally look up during change to see if the top leaders are serious about it and actually leading the way. Do the leaders' actions demonstrate commitment? Are measurements in place for the organization, teams, and individuals? Have the leaders reprioritized to put emphasis on the change? The leader's shadow is long and can either cast a great doubt in employees' minds or can inspire confidence and assurance that change is going to happen.

A few years ago, we worked with two senior leaders in different companies, both dealing with large-scale change, who got significantly different results. To protect their identities, we'll call them Mica and Damian. Both of these leaders were responsible for thousands of people and millions of dollars in revenue. Both leaders needed to compel their senior teams and directors to quickly and effectively change what was done and how it was done for their businesses to stay vital.

Mica was a former Olympic champion, Harvard educated, aggressive in his sales approach with good results, and had a can-do attitude. All of these characteristics made him a natural, hard-hitting, effective leader (one would think). Mica was meeting his sales goals, but there were negative impacts along the way. His employee-engagement scores were the lowest in the company. The CEO was concerned about the impact of low engagement on retention because Mica's area was so critical to the business. So the CEO asked us to coach both Mica and his team through the next phase of major change. When interviewing his people, we heard the following comments about Mica's leadership: "Intense," "Demanding," "I don't trust him," "Flies off the handle," "Overbearing," and "Obsessive." Not good adjectives to describe a senior leader. Mica knew the business inside and out, but he was alienating his team. His leadership shadow was causing distrust and resentment.

When we started working with Mica, he described himself as stressed out, unhealthy, worried, and unhappy in many aspects of his life. And he felt a lot of pressure to succeed in the business. Historically, Mica had a great relationship with the CEO, who was one of his closest friends when they started the business. But when we met him, Mica wasn't comfortable with the key leaders under him, and he wasn't happy with how his relationships were evolving with cross-functional leaders with whom he often felt competitive.

In short, Mica was in a leadership death spiral (and diving fast). The facets of Mica's leadership shadow (what he said, did, measured, and prioritized) were all linked together and created a picture of how effective he was as a leader. Mica was usually in a reactive mode, often on edge, and typically alienated key stakeholders. He had recently been passed up for a key assignment and promotion. And his opinion (once one of the most valued in the company) was often overlooked.

During our coaching sessions with him, we concentrated on his own resiliency as a leader—his capacity to maintain composure, think clearly, sustain high energy, and focus during the chaos created by change. Mica was burned out and had no reserves to give. So we focused on his health, well-being, relationships, fitness, and even meditation and relaxation. Little by little, he started to ease into a better style, and we could see glimpses of who he had been years ago and why he had ascended to an important leadership position in the first place. Working with him and his team in the turnaround, we talked about the leader's shadow and how he could address incongruences in his approach. His attitude shifted considerably, and so did the results of his team. Eventually, his business unit's employee engagement scores soared.

...

"Knowing others is intelligence. Knowing yourself is true wisdom. Mastering others is strength. Mastering yourself is true power."

—Lao Tzu, *Tao Te Ching*, "The Classic of the Virtuous Way" (Chinese manual on the art of living, and one of the wonders of the world)

Contrast the story of Mica with that of Damian, the GM and Senior VP of a Fortune 50 firm in the United States. We followed him for over five years in three key positions as he led turnarounds in different regions of the country. Each time he was given a new assignment, the region was the lowest or near the lowest of the twelve regions. And each time, after several years of hard work, his region rose to the top in the five most important ratings of the business's success. Like all leaders, Damian cast a long shadow. The difference was that his shadow accelerated change. How were the two leaders different?

Mica's CEO asked us to work to support Mica. Damian, on the other hand, sought us out himself to coach and consult with his team and the business. We have been surprised over the years to see that the most successful leaders we work with in change are often the most proactive and open to learning and growth. Here are some other things we noticed about Damian's approach to leading change:

- A major passion not only for the business, but for people, processes, and leadership

- Relentless in his interest to learn and understand what would motivate his team

- A willingness to try almost anything we suggested to get better results

- A sharp vision for change

- An ability to involve a wide cross-section of stakeholders in the process in meaningful ways

- A commitment to deep analysis to find the root cause issues in the systems and processes that ran the business (nothing was sacred and everyone knew that)

- A focus on his key players—always anticipating their needs and developing them

- An interest in frontline workers demonstrated by regular conversations to understand their perspectives

- The ability to recognize others freely and celebrate success regularly

- A clear priority for both people and results

- Care for his own health and resiliency as a leader

In short, what Damian said, he did. He measured and he prioritized. His shadow grew longer and larger, and the change he was able to lead in each case was extraordinary. To this day, we have never worked with an individual leader who commanded such great respect and appreciation from his people and who achieved such incredible results. Damian's positive leadership shadow accelerated his team toward amazing change.

...

"Immaturity lies only in total ignorance of self. To understand yourself is the beginning of wisdom."

—Krishnamurti, speaker and writer of philosophy

CRITICALITY OF DEVELOPING SELF AND OTHERS

We can't end this discussion about a leader's shadow without focusing attention on the need for leaders to develop themselves. Until a leader changes, not much happens. A leader's transformation is very personal and inside-out. Leading change must focus on leading self and improving your own leadership effectiveness. This is the personal, inner game of change.

Leading change also means investing in the improvement of leadership throughout the organization. Leadership development gives strength to the leadership spine and changes both the capability and capacity of the organization to further transform in the future. When the collective capacity of leaders improves, it creates an updraft that carries the business to greater heights. The opposite can also be true—leaders can create a downdraft that increases drag on the business. What's your impact and what are you doing to improve it?

...

"I am of the opinion that my life belongs to the whole community,
and as long as I live, it is my privilege to do for it whatever I can.
I want to be thoroughly used up when I die, for the harder I work
the more I live. I rejoice in life for its own sake. Life is no
'brief candle' to me. It is a sort of splendid torch which I have
got hold of for a moment, and I want to make it burn as brightly
as possible before handing it on to future generations."

—George Bernard Shaw, Irish playwright, critic,
and Nobel Prize winner in literature

The words of George Bernard Shaw are applicable to leadership development. It is a privilege to lead, and leaders must remember that their shadows impact the entire organization. Your business is your "community." Is your impact more like a small candle glow or a "splendid torch"? Are you helping to improve the collective talent of other leaders? Are you effectively lighting the way for employees and giving them a clear, bright path to follow? Martin Luther King Jr. said, "Faith is taking the first step even when you don't see the whole staircase." Effective leaders of change build that faith in their people so they will not only take the first step, but also climb the whole staircase.

A master teacher and colleague, Bill Adams (who co-authored the book *Mastering Leadership*), brilliantly highlights the need for developing self and others. To help senior leaders understand that they must develop their own capacity and the collective capability and capacity of leaders in the business, he asks a series of questions:

- At what pace is your leadership evolving (at pace with or ahead of the change curve of your industry)?

- How well are you and your leaders staying up with the escalating complexity of your business?

- How effective are you as a leader? How do you know?

- Is your inner game matched to the scope and complexity of the environment you are in? If not, where do you need to up your game?

- Where do you need to upgrade your leadership influence? How is this impacting your leadership conversations?

- What is the effectiveness of your leadership development system? How do you know? What are you doing to actively enhance the effectiveness of leaders?

- What is the return on your leadership system?

How comfortable are you with your answers? Most of the leaders we have worked with have never considered these poignant questions. And yet the impact is either monumental or detrimental. As Bob Anderson and Bill Adams say, "The organization cannot perform at a higher level of performance than the collective capability and capacity of your leadership." They also say, "Collective leadership effectiveness drives business performance."[11]

So to get a high-performing culture, leaders must combine an outside-in approach (doing all the things we have previously discussed) with an inside-out approach. This means improving your leadership and the collective leadership of all those in the leadership spine. The combined strength of the leadership shadow will determine the ability to scale the business, improve the customer experience, make effective decisions, and grow the business now and in the future.

Dave Ulrich and Norm Smallwood found significant evidence of the need for effective leaders in their book *Why the Bottom Line ISN'T!* They found that "investor confidence in leadership, employees, and the firm's culture increased market value as much as or more than financial performance."[12] In other words, the value of many firms has as much to do with perceived value as hard assets. The intangible value of leadership has become a tangible, quantifiable market value. As the authors say, "The soft stuff is as important as the hard stuff because it builds customer, investor, and employee confidence about the future."[13] Developing yourself and others is a tangible way to increase value and confidence in the firm and in the change initiative you are leading.

...

> **"The quality of a person's life is in direct proportion**
> **to their commitment to excellence, regardless of**
> **their chosen field of endeavor."**
>
> —Vince Lombardi, considered to be one of the best coaches in NFL history

Consequently, "changing how you change" has to include changing leadership. Indeed, nothing enduring will happen until it does. Great change leaders focus inwardly and begin their own journey of personal transformation, and then enable other leaders to do the same. Collective leadership effectiveness will light the way and inspire employees to follow.

SUMMARY

We once read, "One cannot lead others at a higher level than one is leading oneself." Leading change is an inside-out endeavor first. Leaders must push themselves to think and act differently—to be the change they expect in others. Then leading change becomes an outside-in adventure. As the leader grows, so too does the change. People at the top of the chain actually lead the effort, not just manage it; they remove barriers for others; they activate the leadership spine, focusing particularly on mid-level managers; and they ensure the shadows they are casting on the organization accelerate the change. Without leadership, the most elegant vision and most carefully detailed plans have a 50/50 chance of success, at best. With strong leadership, imperfect change plans and clunky implementation can still yield results because the nature of leadership accelerates change.

CHAPTER SUMMARY

KEY POINTS

- One of the biggest derailers we have seen in good leaders is their inability to lead themselves, their organization, their team, their peers, and even their boss. This leads to a lack of scale and inability to leverage, and it hampers the organization's capacity to grow.

- Organizations that value interactions among leaders have twice the leader experience as competitors, three and a half times the leadership bench strength, twice the financial impact, and 20% more leaders ready to fill critical roles—all of which are important to getting change implemented effectively and growing the business.

- If you don't have (or are not investing in) capital in the relationship bank accounts of the people who need to support the change, the change initiative will be bankrupt.

- The behaviors and actions of a leader are critical elements in change. You must be the change you seek in others.

- In the managing change approach, the paradigm of the leader is to make easy moves that apply outside-in drivers to the system to compel change. In the leading change approach, the leader seeks to understand and eliminate the four underlying barriers—the restraining coils—in the system that prevent the organization from changing—including mistrust, lack of clarity, low engagement, and organizational misalignments.

- Managers of change ask other people to figure it out. Leaders of change work with others to figure it out. Managers are only mildly involved. Leaders are intimately involved. Managers rubber-stamp the goals. Leaders work hard to make sure the goals are right and shared. Managers want a quick fix. Leaders know it will likely take time. Managers push on drivers, such as layoffs and pay cuts. Leaders remove restraining barriers.

- Leaders of change never disengage from the process until the change is successfully implemented.

- To accelerate change and increase their odds of success, effective leaders of change engage and empower the leadership spine starting with the CEO and moving down to directors, managers, and supervisors.

- Leading change must focus on leading self and improving your own leadership effectiveness. This is the personal, inner game of change. In addition, leadership development requires investing in the improvement of collective leadership effectiveness throughout the organization.

- The combined strength of all of the leaders' shadows will determine the ability to scale the business; the potential for a business to perform better in the future; whether the customer experience will be improved; the way decisions are made; and ultimately whether a company can change at or above the speed of change to ensure survival.

6

ENSURING SUSTAINABILITY

**"If you have built castles in the air, your work
need not be lost; that is where they should be.
Now put the foundations under them."**

—Henry David Thoreau, American author, poet, and philosopher

n the early 1990s, PepsiCo rolled out a new soft drink called Crystal Pepsi. The idea was to introduce a clear-colored, healthier drink into the cola wars. After positive consumer tests in select markets, the company launched the new soft drink nationwide in the United States. The product utterly failed in spite of PepsiCo's best plans and efforts. Today, case studies and lists of new product failures showcase Crystal Pepsi as a prime example of a big fail. (It's interesting to note that shortly after the launch of Crystal Pepsi, Coca-Cola introduced a similar product called Tab Clear, which met an identical fate.)

What caused Crystal Pepsi to fail? Was it taste? Likely. It's hard to carve out space in an established industry. David C. Novak, chairman of Yum Brands (the corporation that owns PepsiCo), is credited with introducing the Crystal Pepsi concept. He said, "It would have been nice if I'd made sure the product tasted good." Was it the marketing? Hard to say. Pepsi launched a large marketing campaign that included bus-wrapped ads, a Van Halen hit song titled "Right Now" that aired during the Super Bowl, and full-sized sample bottles with the Sunday newspaper in select areas of the country. Did the company misunderstand consumers, given the initial positive sales of $474 million? Easy to do, especially if the first-year sales were driven more out of curiosity than preference. The reason for the failure was likely a combination of these factors that quickly doomed the new product. But interestingly, Novak made the following statement in a December 2007 interview:

> It was a tremendous learning experience. I still think it's the best idea I ever had, and the worst executed. A lot of times as a leader you think, "They don't get it; they don't see my vision." People were saying we should stop and address some issues along the way, and they were right. Once you have a great idea and you blow it, you don't get a chance to resurrect it.[1]

How many great ideas are you trying to implement and sustain? Are your change recommendations being received like Crystal Pepsi? Are people bringing up issues that you aren't willing to address? Are your stakeholders confused? Are your employees not "getting it"? What's the risk of your initiative suffering the same fate as Crystal Pepsi and your business performance declining?

A McKinsey & Company global study called "Why Implementation Matters," conducted in 2014, found the following:

> Good implementers—defined as companies where respondents reported top-quartile scores for their implementation capabilities—are 4.7 times more likely than those at the bottom-quartile companies to say they ran successful change efforts over the past 5 years. Respondents at the good implementers also score their companies around 30% higher on a series of financial performance

indexes. Perhaps most important, the good-implementer respondents say their companies sustained twice the value from their prioritized opportunities 2 years after the change efforts ended, compared with those at poor implementers.[2]

The head of the change office at one of our long-term clients has five hundred to seven hundred corporate change initiatives that he's responsible for tracking and coordinating. Clearly, that is too many to be effective, and he is trying to prioritize those down to a manageable number. As part of that process, he discovered two things. First, many of their initiatives are "on the books" to deliver results like cost savings, efficiencies, or improvements in operations. But the company is not getting the three- to five-year return on the investment (ROI) from these projects that was calculated during the analysis phase. Why not?

The second finding is that nobody is managing the implementation, clearing roadblocks, or ensuring that stakeholders aren't confused about each of these initiatives. Instead, change teams do the analysis, build the recommendations, and get approval. Then they throw all of that over the wall to Operations. The change team disengages from the process and expects Operations to establish the new norm and achieve the ROI. It feels like a modern-day Crystal Pepsi experience—lots of good ideas with lousy implementation. No wonder the ROI for the portfolio of change projects falls far short of expectations!

Whether you're trying to change consumer tastes or simply modify a company procedure, you must tackle the details of implementation and sustainability or you won't get the desired results. We know this isn't easy. Most organizations have to pull off incredible juggling acts, and they have too many competing priorities and too few resources to keep all the change "balls" in the air without dropping a few. So how can you get through the long, often tedious process of change to the point where you actually see the business results you are hoping for? Think about this story. An air traffic controller was asked how the Chicago airport could land so many planes at once, to which he responded, "One plane at a time." That's the secret to sustainability—you have to land each change project one at a time. And that includes doing a few things after landing, such as taxiing to the gate, securing the jet bridge, and making sure everyone knows where they are going next.

In this chapter, we will describe some common rollout failure paths to avoid when implementing change. Then we will share four disciplines to ensure long-term sustainability of change and to get the desired Return on Investment.

...

"A genuine leader is not a searcher for consensus,
but a molder of consensus."

—Martin Luther King Jr., American activist and humanitarian

NOT THIS WAY: TEN COMMON FAILURE PATHS TO AVOID

In 1996, Harvard Business School professor John Kotter claimed that nearly 70% of large-scale change programs didn't meet their goals,[3] and many surveys since have uncovered similar results. In a recent article by change guru Gary Hamel about why change efforts fail, he said,

> Traditional change programs fail to harness the discretionary creativity and energy of employees and often generate cynicism and resistance. Senior executives talk about the need to get buy-in, but genuine buy-in is the product of involvement, not slick packaging and communication. To be embraced, a change effort must be socially constructed in a process that gives everyone the right to set priorities, diagnose barriers, and generate options. Despite assertions to the contrary, people aren't against change—they are against royal edicts.[4]

When we shared the dismal change success rate with some of our clients in the oil industry and asked how it applied to them, they said, "We don't manage the rollout of the change. We don't plan for it; we don't train people how to do it; we don't stick around to implement; and we don't coordinate it." We see this same pattern with other clients. The planning goes well, but the sustainment falls flat.

We don't want that to happen to you. We want you to nail the rollout and sustain the changes in a way that gets you the performance you're looking for. To do that, you have to avoid these ten common failure paths that we've seen time and time again. These are traps that will ruin all of your hard work and effort.

1. **"We don't need an implementation team."** Yes, you do. You absolutely need a team of people to manage the change plan, including communication, involvement, education, etc., during the later phases of the project. Gary Hamel asserts, "In most organizations, change is regarded as an episodic interruption of the status quo."[5] We know of one leader who brought everyone together and announced the changes but didn't appoint a group to work through the details of the change, such as the new roles, the decision hierarchy, work processes, etc. Guess how well that announcement changed the status quo. Not at all! If an implementation team (or a business operating team) isn't established to work through all the details not accounted for in the original change vision, employees will treat it like an interruption to their work and just wait for it to go away.

2. **"Everyone will just get it done."** No one is going to get the change done if you haven't established clear roles, responsibilities, and accountabilities for the results. In *Decide and Deliver*, our colleague Marcia Blenko says that role clarity is one of the top factors contributing to decision effectiveness and organizational performance. From start to finish, people need to

know their roles, their responsibilities, and what results will be expected of them. And then, leaders need to follow through and hold people accountable for those expectations.

...

"Desire is the key to motivation, but it's determination and commitment to an unrelenting pursuit of your goal—a commitment to excellence—that will enable you to attain the success you seek."

—Mario Andretti, Italian-American world champion racing driver

3.   **"We don't need to involve so many people."** The more people you involve, the better, as long as their efforts are coordinated and focused toward the same goal. Large change projects often require the work of many sub-project teams. These mini change teams are a great way to boost involvement and commitment and get fresh perspectives. See Appendix 2 for an example of questions and deliverables at each phase of a change project to ensure involvement and commitment.

4.   **"Timing and sequencing don't really matter."** The sequence of rollout events can actually make or break a change. One of our clients tells the story of managing the rollout of new SAP software. The size and complexity of the project was enormous given their global scale and diversity of sites. Right in the middle of this project, new Y2K requirements emerged and suddenly became the top priority. The SAP rollout had to be reprioritized and scaled back, something that wouldn't have needed to happen if the sequencing of change had been better managed.

5.   **"Do more with less."** Change projects require time, attention, money, and people. The bigger the vision and goal, the more resources you'll need. Big goals plus few resources usually equals failure. We understand that some companies are

operating on very narrow margins and don't have a lot to throw at a change project. In this case, you'll likely have to lower your expectations of what you can realistically achieve. Remember our newspaper client that we mentioned earlier? They originally had two goals: keep the print side of the business profitable and expand their online presence. But the goals ended up cannibalizing each other. The funds needed to create new print products were also needed to develop a more significant Internet offering. And the creative, experienced people needed on the print side of the business were the same ones needed on the online side of the business. The consequence was predictable and devastating. Neither goal achieved success fast enough. When we came into the picture, they wanted help with a new change project—dramatically downsizing the business to reduce costs and then working their way back from there.

6. **"Everyone should work in their own functional area."** Working in silos by failing to coordinate the many interrelationships among mini change teams and other changes that are being implemented simultaneously is disastrous. One of our clients in an online marketing and sales business bought four of its smaller competitors to build the brand and create an even greater online presence for buyers. Initially, the leadership team wanted to leave the smaller companies alone and allow them to operate somewhat independently given their great individual track records. But investors became frustrated when the consolidation didn't produce any savings. So the executive team rolled out four key initiatives for all businesses that were designed to preserve the core of what made each business great while finding synergies among the units. It was a great idea, just like Crystal Pepsi. And also like Crystal Pepsi, the execution was terrible. The four initiatives were rolled out without any oversight or cross-coordination. Many of the businesses were

in the middle of their own change projects and had no idea how these four initiatives melded with what they were already doing. Results took a dip as workers tried to do everything at once. Finally, after some very candid leadership conversations about the issues, the silos began to break down. They were then able to coordinate their various projects and gain some traction around the four initiatives.

7. **"We don't need to measure. We'll know it when we see it."** Often the original goal of the change project gets lost in the translation of implementation. Keeping the focus on goals and measuring regularly toward that end seems almost too obvious to mention. But we often find that organizations lose sight of the vision, the business case, and the ultimate results they were shooting for because of poor execution. Is it any wonder that so many change efforts fail to achieve their desired results when no one is tracking and managing toward those results? Unless someone is paying careful attention, the desired results will never show up on the company scorecard or the company ledger in any meaningful way.

...

"There is a difference between interest and commitment. When you're interested in doing something, you do it only when it's convenient. When you're committed to something, you accept no excuses, only results."

—Ken Blanchard, American author and management expert

8. **"We need to just stick with the plan."** It shouldn't surprise you that changes happen during change projects. Issues arise that no one could have anticipated during the planning stage. Someone has to be responsible for modifications and adaptations

during rollout because they will arise. Years ago, we were part of an organization that merged with another firm. Our executive team asked us to help integrate the two businesses. From a strategic level, the merger was the right move, and many clients and analysts applauded the deal. But some challenges arose from a tactical perspective. During the transition process, some teams were required to move to the new headquarters. The dress code at the new location was vastly different from the dress code at their old office. Significant? For some it became a huge issue. In one part of the organization, they had been required to wear ties and dress shirts for men and business attire for women. In another part of the organization, they had groups that wore shorts and flip-flops. We were surprised to discover that some employees refused to move office locations because of the dress codes. We look back now and laugh that this was such an issue. But beliefs ran deep in both organizations, and mantras like "you act how you dress" were flung around. For the executives, it became a defining moment as they listened to employees and established the new culture of the combined firms. The dress code was modified, and the teams finally agreed to relocate. The point is that no one planned on this happening. Someone had to make modifications and adjustments to avoid a derailment.

9. **"Once we 'go live,' people will figure it out and adjust."** Inherent in change is transition—for customers, people, technology, processes, and systems. In the book *Fake Work*, our colleagues Gaylan Nielson and Brent Peterson cite a study by Harris Group Poll that found 51% of workers don't understand what they need to do to execute on the goals and priorities, 73% of workers say their organizations' strategies and goals are not translated into specific work tasks they can execute, and 70% of workers do not know what to do to support their

organizations' strategies and goals. If these numbers are representative of your firm, it could cripple your implementation of change. Change requires seeing people and things through the needed transitions. In *Managing Transitions*, William Bridges taught that people have to work through three phases: (1) endings, (2) neutral, and (3) beginnings. Failure to enable these transitions will only prolong the status quo and reduce the likelihood of achieving quantifiable results.

...

"Nothing so undermines organizational change as the failure to think through who will have to let go of what when change occurs."

—William Bridges, American author, speaker, and organizational consultant

10. **"We'll celebrate when we see the end result."** You should always stay focused on the end result, but small victories along the way are important to recognize and celebrate. Years ago, we were asked to help a military command with its primary mission to make ready and deploy reserve units to the front. During the change team's analysis, we discovered that units weren't fully deployable because they didn't have the following:

- Available and qualified soldiers (not enough recruited or trained)

- Enough of the right equipment on hand

- Family care plans in place

- Up-to-date physical and dental profiles or security clearances

- Weapon qualifications

As you might expect, these weren't easy things to fix. The long-term result was to create a balanced scorecard complete with lead and lag measures that would help them understand and improve their deployability index. We also identified some short-term goals that they could achieve quickly and inexpensively to get some traction. These short-term wins included the following:

- Focusing on family support during mobilizations (e.g., making sure paychecks went to the right place so families could pay the rent while their loved ones were deployed)

- Creating a process to manage inactive duty training participation

- Establishing mentoring and counseling programs

- Adding more mechanics to keep equipment maintained

We immediately communicated, achieved, and celebrated these quick wins. The short-term goals were the levers that enabled us to make progress toward the strategic priorities. Once the soldiers could see that we cared about their welfare inherent in the quick wins, they were more committed and passionate to help the organization achieve its mission-critical goals.

YOUR ROAD TO ROLLOUT

How well you're avoiding the ten failure paths of rollout is a good indicator of the ultimate success of your change project. We assess each of the ten failure paths with our clients using the following rating system:

1 = We are avoiding this failure path entirely.

2 = We are veering slightly toward this failure path, and we have solutions in place to course-correct.

3 = We are on this failure path, and we have a solid plan in place to get off it.

4 = We are on this failure path, and we don't know what to do to get off it.

5 = We are on this failure path, and the change is derailed because of it.

The higher your score, the higher the likelihood that your change is going to fail.

...

"The key to being a successful skipper is to see the ship through the eyes of the crew. Only then can you find what's really wrong and, in so doing, help the sailors empower themselves to fix it."

—Captain D. Michael Abrashoff, former commander of USS *Benfold*

MAKING CHANGE STICK

Institutionalizing change is perhaps one of the most difficult leadership challenges that executives encounter in their professional lives. For example, think about a time in your personal life when you changed something—a behavior, a habit, your weight, etc. Were you able to sustain that change for a year or more? What was it about the dynamics of that situation that allowed the change to last?

We have asked these questions to hundreds of participants in our leading change courses, and the personal stories and examples are amazing and significant. However, it is equally amazing how few people can say they have experienced lasting personal or professional change. More often than not, participants can think of only one or two examples from an entire life.

What makes change stick? Clients have told us they sustained a personal change because of high motivation, a serious rationale (e.g., life or death health issue), a clear goal, visible measures of success, and consistent accountability. Alan Deutschman's bestseller *Change or Die* outlines three keys to sustaining change (sometimes called the three Rs):

- **Relate**: New hope—a new emotional relationship is formed with a person or community that inspires and sustains hope.

- **Repeat**: New skills—the new relationship helps you learn, practice, and master the new habits and skills that you'll need.

- **Reframe**: New thinking—the new relationship helps you learn new ways of thinking about your situation and your life.

The first key to creating sustainable change, **Relate**, is rooted in psychology research that confirms that learning is a social process. When human beings are involved in change and learning, it is usually more successful in social settings where other people can support. For example, someone trying to lose weight might seek the support of an organization like Weight Watchers. The group consists of likeminded people who set goals, meet weekly to check progress, share best practices, and motivate each other to succeed. The technical aspect of this first key turns out to be much less important than the regular social support. In any change situation, personal or professional, the idea of relating to others is critical. Meaningful involvement in change and connecting with others who are also moving through the change helps people believe that the future state will be better than the status quo.

The second key to sustaining change, **Repeat**, is grounded in neuroscience research. Studies on stroke patients who have lost the use of their motor function show that repetition can reactivate the motor skills. New neuropathways are formed to bypass the damaged areas of the brain, and patients can achieve a certain level of mobility. Similarly, during times of change in a business setting, individuals and teams create new pathways (e.g., work processes, procedures, communication, etc.) for the new required behaviors. Leaders engage in consistent, repetitive communication to remind people of the goals, business case, work structure changes, and behavioral changes. When people know what is expected and what to do, and that message is repeated and reinforced all around them in various ways, change happens.

The third key to sustainable change is **Reframe**. Most people, when dealing with significant change, "take the facts and fit them into the frames [paradigms or beliefs] they already have. If the facts don't fit, they're likely to challenge whether they're really facts or to dismiss the information and persist somehow in believing what they want to believe."[6] For example, Deutschman documented in his book a study of 37,000 patients who had suffered a major heart attack and were prescribed heart medication; nearly everyone took the pills for the first month or two, but half of the patients stopped taking them at the three-month mark. One year later, only one-fifth of the patients were still taking their prescribed medication. Taking daily medication simply didn't fit into the frame of these patients' lives, so the change didn't stick. However, a few clinics have had success working with the same types of patients. These clinics have been able to help the patients reframe their lifestyles in a way that incorporates the medication as part of a healthy routine. Changes in business follow the same pattern. When leaders help employees reframe the change in positive ways for their work and career progression, the new required behaviors are more likely to stick and the transformation be achieved.

...

"All great changes are preceded by chaos."

—Deepak Chopra, Indian-American author and public speaker

LIFT AND DRAG

Many years ago, Tony and his wife, Teresa, lived in rural Connecticut on a farm at the top of a large and beautiful hill in the foothills of the Berkshire Mountains. In the fall, they would often awaken to a loud hissing noise in the early morning hours as multicolored hot air balloons with enthusiastic leaf watchers swooped over the homestead. Sometimes the leaf peepers would drop anchor in their field and share picnics and libations with them as tribute for the landing site.

During this time, Teresa became smitten with the idea of hot air ballooning and wanted to take a ride for their upcoming wedding anniversary. To her, a balloon ride was a fun and romantic idea; for Tony, it was terrifying because of his fear of heights and small places. The thought of being thousands of feet in the air in a small basket tethered to a balloon rising as a result of fire heating a fabric container was petrifying! The similarities between Tony's anxiety about hot air ballooning and what employees feel during change are too rich to go unmentioned. Some employees are excited about the idea of change; some are terrified. Some find the ride exhilarating, while others find it paralyzing. Some people will jump right in the basket and look forward to the journey and the destination. Others will have to be slowly coaxed into the basket and constantly reminded about why they are there in the first place and where they are going.

After doing some additional research to see if his fears about hot air ballooning were warranted, Tony discovered other similarities to change. A hot air balloon gets lift when the air temperature inside the envelope makes it lighter than the surrounding (ambient) air. The lift or float happens because of the buoyant force exerted on it. (This force is described by Archimedes' principle and also happens when objects float in water.) The amount of lift (or buoyancy) provided by a hot air balloon depends primarily upon the difference between the temperature of the air inside the envelope and the temperature of the air outside the envelope.

Now let's apply this concept to change. For your change to float and stay in the air, you need to generate more heat inside the initiatve than is outside in the surrounding environment. If you don't, your change won't have lift.

...

"Some people change when they see the light,
others when they feel the heat."

–Caroline Schroeder, associate professor, Religious and
Classical Studies, the University of the Pacific

So what creates lift? What propels the change forward? To launch and sustain a change, you've got to turn up the heat! All of the things we've discussed in these chapters—the vision, leadership, engagement, and alignment activities—will generate the necessary heat to lift your change. It's equally important to think about what creates drag. Typical reasons we've seen for change to lose momentum include competing demands, lack of defined success, rewards for old behavior, and insufficient resources.

FOUR DISCIPLINES TO ENSURE LONG-TERM SUSTAINABILITY OF CHANGE

After a lot of trial and error, we have found that the following four disciplines enable leaders to generate lift and sustain change. These disciplines will reframe reality for your employees and increase the probability that your change will stick:

1. Validate project readiness
2. Hand off the project to the business
3. Create a discipline of accountability
4. Establish learning and renewal

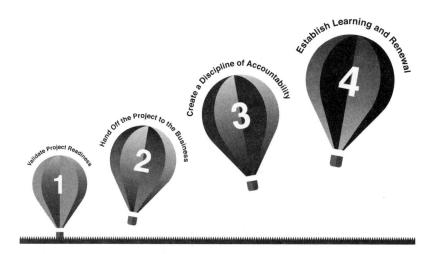

1. Validate Project Readiness

...

"To be prepared is half the victory."

—Miguel de Cervantes Saavedra, Spanish novelist, poet, and playwright

The first discipline of successful sustainability is validating project readiness. Up to this point in the project, leaders have spent time getting the technical aspects of the change in place (i.e., the business of transforming the business). Some implementation has already occurred or is in progress in key areas, such as aligning business processes, engaging employees, and making changes to systems. Validating project readiness is a quick check to ensure all systems are ready for the change team to pass the project to the business. This step validates the readiness of leadership to lead and stakeholders to receive the change.

We recently worked with a Fortune 500 business that engaged us to build change capability in their organization. When we started the project, the business was thriving. Within six months, the entire local and global industry had been upended. In the beginning, our client thought they were ready to change. But by the time we handed the project over to the business to operate, so many factors had shifted that the readiness quotient plunged to almost zero!

While this is an extreme example, we have seen many similar situations. Change leaders complete tremendous amounts of work that we have described in the previous chapters. They feel good about their plans and have already implemented many changes, but employees too often aren't ready for their role in implementation when it comes. It's important to ensure involvement and commitment at every step along the way—from vision through to implementation. But in case you haven't done that thoroughly or missed involving a critical group at some point, now is the time to complete an all-systems check on readiness. Find out which areas or stakeholders need more focus to enable lift and avoid drag for the project.

Below are project readiness questions that we use to make a cursory assessment. We call this the Baker's Dozen of Project Readiness. After so much work has been put into the change, it's tempting to simply check off this list with a quick yes, yes, yes. But we would encourage you to think carefully about these questions to ensure the project is truly ready for lift off.

BAKER'S DOZEN OF PROJECT READINESS

1. Is there a compelling case for change that is well understood?

2. Are plans and expectations clear? Do employees know what behaviors and actions are required of them?

3. Are measures of success in place and ready to be monitored on a consistent, timely basis?

4. Were key stakeholders involved in creating the solution? Has resistance been dealt with openly?

5. Is the leadership spine aligned and strong?

6. Are leaders modeling the change?

7. Are processes, structure, and systems aligned to support the change?

8. Has the culture been enabled to support the change?

9. Has the right training been provided to meet new capability requirements of employees?

10. Have employees been engaged in meaningful discussions about the change?

11. Does the change team continue to meet on a frequent basis? Are members following through on assignments?

12. Are quick wins being celebrated to create momentum for the change among the employee population?

13. Is there a process in place to review the effectiveness of the project implementation and to learn from both successes and failures?

Validating project readiness is our version of a preflight check to ensure all systems are working and everyone is on board and engaged. Only then should the change team hand off the project to the business for implementation.

2. Hand Off the Project to the Business

...

"Nothing diminishes anxiety faster than action."

–Walter Anderson, American painter, writer, and naturalist

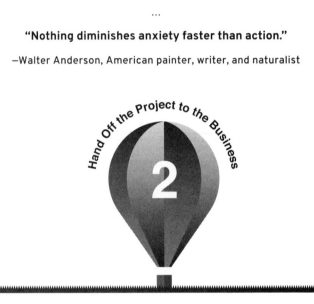

The second discipline of sustainability is handing off the project to the business operating team. Ideally, the business has been involved in the project all along. Sometimes at large corporations, however, a change team is set up separate from the business operating team so the business can continue to run. This step is to ensure that the business operating team is ready to take ownership of the change, continue implementing the plan, and weave the changes into the fabric of the business.

Recently we worked with a retail operation that was attempting to infuse some creative and innovative thinking into the change process to transform from a purely physical retailer to a virtual retailer. Many of the leaders in the company were from a traditional mindset, and they wanted to minimize their vulnerability in the normal streams of business. So they decided to break off a group of more innovative executives and have them work on the change independent of the operations group. (Warning flags and sirens should be going off in your mind.) Their hope was to mitigate losses while still changing the business. The innovation team did some great work, but it failed to include the operations team in the process and thinking. The result was a disastrous handoff. It didn't matter how wonderful the ideas were from the innovation team; the fact that the operations team had no buy-in or link to the change doomed the change to failure.

Three factors can help make the handoff successful:

RECONNECT WITH THE VISION

- Reconnect with the vision of success established in the beginning. Too many projects drag on indefinitely only to suffer a slow and painful death. Be clear on what success will look like, and be ready to stop something that isn't working.

- Reengage with the sponsor team. Make sure they continue to allocate time on their calendars to ensure the success of the project.

ENSURE DISCIPLINE IN IMPLEMENTATION

- Revise rollout plans from the plan phase according to any changes in the schedule of the business.

- Transition project responsibilities.

    ◦ Transition ownership of the plan to the business.
    ◦ Begin meeting together (the change team with the business operating team).
    ◦ Transition responsibilities and accountabilities.

- Roll out the business measures and track progress.
  - Share lead and lag measures.
  - Share how to evaluate results against goals for each team.
  - Hold leaders and teams responsible for measuring.
  - Make sure employees know what they need to be doing differently.

- Assign oversight for realigning the processes, structure, and system changes.

- Highlight cultural and psychological restraining forces and the plans to overcome them.

TRANSITION THE PROJECT TO THE BUSINESS OPERATING TEAM

- Identify the business sponsor.

- Update work processes, structure, and systems to align with the change.

- Revise the performance management descriptions to foster the new behaviors.

- Track new business measures.

- Build learning and development systems so employees develop desired behaviors and skills.

- Conduct closure meetings and ceremonies to communicate the handoff.

Someone once said, "A sure path to failure in change is to keep your hands off during the handoff!" The change team must hold tight to the change until it is safely in the hands of the business and moving forward.

3. Create a Discipline of Accountability

...

**"Continuous effort—not strength or intelligence—
is the key to unlocking our potential."**

–Liane Cordes, author

The third practice that leads to successful sustainability of projects is to create a discipline of accountability. For many of our clients, this is the hardest part of the overall change process. Most businesses run at such a fast pace there is little time to focus on this practice. Usually we see leaders who find it much easier to let the project go and hope for great success rather than create a discipline of accountability. But as it's been said, "Hope is not a strategy."

Years ago we were hired to run a change project for a major financial service organization in New York. The organization found that about 70% of its overall business came from about 10% of the top sales reps in the United States. The goal of the change project was to understand what made the top performers so great and to create an environment for the majority of the sales force (some five thousand people) to become equally successful. We researched the situation and identified some areas for process improvements that would better enable the sales group.

Sales managers throughout the business were trained on these improvements and coached on how to ensure follow-through and accountability. The effort could have been considered a success at that point given that all major milestones were completed. But when it comes to change, it's not the milestones we're after. It's the results! The project was done, but was the sales force at large better at generating business? The senior leadership group at the company was so focused on sustainment that they created weekly stand-up meetings with the sales teams to find out if they had really made a change. Each team had its own dashboard that summarized lead and lag measures, overall proficiency, speed of adoption, and utilization of the new skills. During these weekly meetings, they followed a simple yet powerful agenda:

- What happened last week? What were our results?

- What did we learn? What coaching or feedback do we have for each other?

- What will we do differently next week to move the needle in a positive direction? What will each of us commit to do this coming week?

- What support do we need from each other this week to be successful?

The result for our client? The entire sales force stayed focused on raising the level of sales productivity because of this sustainment and accountability process. Within six months, the company saw a spike in revenue of nearly 30%. And maybe more importantly, the company and the sales force institutionalized a set of new skills and a disciplined culture that they have benefited from for many years.

If you want to create a strong discipline of accountability, here are the activities you need to implement:

- Create a dashboard of lead and lag measures.

- Hold a weekly thirty-minute review meeting (e.g., stand-up meeting) with the people responsible for the work on the dashboard.

- Discuss and report on these questions:

  ○ What happened last week? What were our results?
  ○ What did we learn? What coaching or feedback do we have for each other?
  ○ What will we do differently next week to move the needle in a positive direction? What will each of us commit to do this coming week?
  ○ What support do we need from each other this week to be successful?

- Assign ownership.

- Hold people accountable every week.

- Institutionalize cultural behaviors.

Creating a discipline of accountability has a huge impact on achieving and sustaining the change goals. We have found that it's one of the greatest levers a leader can pull to embed change in the fabric of an organization.[7]

4. Establish Learning and Renewal

...

**"Education is the most powerful weapon
you can use to change the world."**

—Nelson Mandela, anti-apartheid revolutionary, philanthropist,
and former president of South Africa

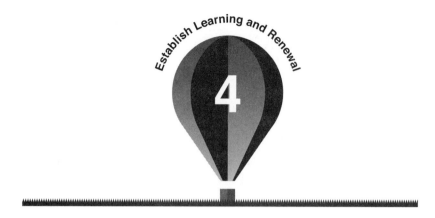

The fourth discipline of successful sustainability is to establish a process of learning and renewal. This practice usually gets the least amount of attention. Many of our clients use so much energy, time, and resources pushing through the initial design and execution of the change effort that there isn't anything left for learning and renewal. Very seldom do leaders assess what worked and what didn't. The practice of capturing learning and celebrating success seems to be a luxury, at first glance. But in reality, it's as critical to the business's long-term success as any substantial accomplishment might be.

Stephen R. Covey brilliantly taught that true effectiveness comes from the balance of *performance* (outcomes) and *performance capability* (ability to produce outcomes in the future). The idea is to build the capability that will allow you to generate results over and over again. We learn this same concept from the fable of the goose and the golden egg. In the story, the farmer discovers that his goose lays golden eggs. At first, he's content to gather one golden egg a day. But he soon becomes greedy and kills the goose in an attempt to get all of the golden eggs at once, thereby killing the producer of the eggs and his chances of long-term wealth in one fell blow. Businesses run the same risk if they don't take time to learn and celebrate. Don't be so anxious to rush off to the next project that you fail to recognize all of the vital contributors to the current success and reflect on what you might do better next time. Taking time to learn and renew allows the acquired knowledge from one project to be woven into the fabric of the culture and dispersed to many future projects.

High-performing businesses take the time to drive success deeper into the business through the discipline of learning and renewal. Helpful learning mechanisms include the following:

- Benchmarking visits

- Customer research

- Scanning the environment; scanning other areas of the business

- Reflections and lessons learned

- Tours and reports

- Stories from employees

- Leader-led breakfasts or brown bag lunches

- All-company reviews

- Pilots

- Action research

- Personnel rotations

A number of years ago, we were hired by a major utility in the Southeast. This particular company was a top performer in its field, but deregulation was creating a different type of competition. Company leaders were attempting to overhaul the entire business in a proactive move to reposition the organization and compete against larger utilities. Because of their preemptive approach, they allowed themselves two years to make the change (a luxury most companies don't have). The result was near-perfect assessment, planning, implementation, and sustainment phases. As part of learning and renewal, leaders took the time to understand what was working well and how it could work even better. They created simple yet impactful learning packets to share with the culture. For example, they captured learnings and actions needed for next time, shared learnings over a website, created a video documenting progress, and documented and standardized processes and actions. The business continues to thrive today due, in part, to the learning and renewal culture leaders created during this massive change effort.

SUMMARY

Sustaining change is hard work. We understand that keeping your change balloon in the air is a tough proposition sometimes. You may get a good liftoff, but then unexpected resistance drags you down. In those moments, the leadership spine must engage to remind people of the reason you are changing and why. You'll need to rekindle the initial sparks that people had for the change in the beginning. As you validate project readiness, create a smooth handoff, institute a discipline of accountability, and continually learn and renew, your change project will soar as you intended it to. The new behaviors will integrate into the culture of the organization and sustain your success now and in the future.

CHAPTER SUMMARY

KEY POINTS

- A common failure of leaders is to not manage the rollout of the change. They don't plan for it; they don't train people how to do it; they don't stick around to implement it; and they don't coordinate it. In short, the planning goes well, but the sustainment falls flat.

- If an implementation team isn't established to work through all the details not accounted for in the original change vision, employees will treat it like an interruption to their work and just wait for it to go away.

- The bigger the vision and goal, the more resources you'll need. Big goals plus few resources usually equals failure.

- We often find that organizations lose sight of the vision, the business case, and the ultimate results they were shooting for during execution. Unless someone is paying careful attention, the desired results will never show up on the company scorecard or the company ledger in any meaningful way.

- Inherent in change is transition—for customers, people, technology, processes, and systems. Failure to enable these transitions will only prolong the status quo and reduce the likelihood of achieving quantifiable results.

- It is important to recognize and celebrate small victories along the way to fuel hope and commitment while waiting for long-term wins.

- Sustaining change requires new emotional relationships that inspire hope, new skills that enable behavior change, and new thinking to reframe "how things are done around here."

- Validating project readiness is a quick check to ensure all systems are ready for the change team to pass the project to the business. This step validates the readiness of leadership to lead and stakeholders to receive the change.

- The change team must hold tight to the change until it is safely in the hands of the business operating team that is ready to take ownership of the change, continue implementing the plan, and weave the changes into the fabric of the business.

- High-performing leaders take time to drive success deeper into the business through the disciplines of assessing readiness, handing off the change to the business, ensuring accountability, and learning and renewing.

ACCELERATING YOUR LEADERSHIP OF CHANGE

"Our moral responsibility is not to stop the future, but to shape it . . . to channel our destiny in humane directions and to ease the trauma of transition."

—Alvin Toffler, American futurist

B
ecoming a master of leading change is one of the most important skills of effective leaders. Leaders have a responsibility to improve business performance, shape how change happens, and deepen both their skills and the collective ability of their people to change. When leaders change the organizational systems and encourage individual behavior change, they ease the trauma of transition that many employees feel during times of upheaval. Leading change is a complex behavioral skillset that requires acumen, practice, and discipline. American entrepreneur and author Jim Rohn is credited with saying, "Success is neither magical nor mysterious. Success is the natural consequence of consistently applying basic fundamentals."

If we are to reverse the 70% fail rate of most change initiatives, it will require both practice and discipline to apply change principles that work. If the task feels daunting, we assure you that the payoff is equally great. Turning around a business, leading a successful change initiative within your team, or helping people move from understanding to commitment to action in a change that affects their career and their life has both extrinsic, business performance benefits as well as intrinsic, personal satisfaction.

LESSONS FROM THE FIELD

We want to conclude with learnings from the field. Below are some case studies from leaders who have been where you are and who made some mistakes along the way. To help you accelerate your change leadership acumen and transform your business, we'll outline some common challenges and tips to solve them.

Client Case #1: Internet-Based Marketing and Advertising Company (where the capacity of the leadership team became the decelerator to growth)

This company was a leader in the online advertising space that grew quickly from an Internet startup to a billion-dollar company. It was based on a brilliant concept that transformed the online marketing, sales, and advertising landscape and simultaneously played a major role in the downfall of the print newspaper business. We were called in by the CEO to address leadership ineffectiveness within the C-suite. The group was much too large when we started (fourteen to sixteen members) and lacked alignment around a common vision for the future of the business. Change had happened so quickly and success so immediately that the company had grown into a "beast" that needed care and feeding well beyond the leadership team's capacity. Even though the business was a huge success, the organization's infrastructure and leadership development lagged pathetically behind. The organization's ability to continue to grow was stymied because the executive team was misaligned, lacked the collective capacity to lead the change, and individual leaders lacked the mindset and skill-set to deal with the pace of change.

We started by right-sizing the C-suite team based on needed skills and organizational structure. Then we had significant work to do to collectively define the future strategy and identify changes to support growth. As part of this strategic effort, we uncovered some deep-seated trust and collaboration issues among executives, which created a huge barrier. What surprised us over the two years that we worked with this group was its lack of both individual and team skills to align and grow the business. They struggled to let go of egos and come together for a common purpose. The business didn't suffer from a lack of ideas for growth (it had achieved incredible results), but from the inability of leaders to align around shared goals and direction.

The lesson we learned from this client was that in a fast-paced, high-growth situation, current organizational success isn't enough to fuel long-term results. In these situations, it's critical to build the change capability within the leadership team so that it has the capacity to operate in an ever-changing and more complex environment. This client required both transforming the business *and* accelerating the collective leadership effectiveness. Only focusing on one would have been good, but both were necessary.

...

"Alone we can do so little; together we can do so much."

—Helen Keller, American author, political activist, and lecturer

Client Case #2: Medical Technology Platform Company (where change at three levels is the only sure way to success)

This company is a potential powerhouse in the medical technology sector with an amazing aptitude for finding solutions to some of the most challenging diseases in the world. The company has a great strategy, world-class research, and sound organizational processes and support systems. Unique and varied leadership styles, however, have caused difficulties with effective communication, problem solving, and joint decision-making across mission critical areas of the business.

We were asked to develop leaders and help them work together effectively, essentially an inside-out approach that began with individual leadership development. In the role we were asked to play, we spent time assessing executives' potential to enable the business to succeed, reporting to the board of directors about progress, and tracking quantifiable shifts in leadership behaviors. After a year of work to accelerate leadership, significant gains have been made in some leaders' effectiveness. But the problem still troubling this group is its inability to work together as a team, which has a profound impact on other areas of the business. Working inside-out has built better leaders, but the overall ineffectiveness of the team could hamper organizational growth and ultimate success. Our takeaway from this engagement is that working to build individual leadership capability through coaching and training is a sound investment, but will not likely be sufficient to achieve the business results. This client has proved to us, once again, that working at the individual, team, and organizational levels simultaneously is necessary for sustained success in accelerating results now and in the future.

...

"Our tendency to create heros rarely jibes with the reality that most nontrivial problems require collective solutions."

—Warren G. Bennis, American scholar,
organizational consultant, and author

Client Case #3: Energy Company (where the individual capacity and effectiveness of leaders will stall ongoing success of the business)

This client has a large business in the energy sector due to huge growth over the past ten years with great upside potential to grow even further. The original focus of our work was to improve change acumen among leaders so the company could continue its rapid growth. To this company's credit, leaders realized that change was bigger than individual transitions (although critically important). They also needed an outside-in approach to clarify the strategy, enable an operational redesign, and further shape the culture. As we worked with the team over several months, we experienced barriers time and time again to the change work we were hired to do. These barriers revolved around a lack of individual leadership effectiveness. Consequently, we conducted a 360-degree feedback and began executive coaching and development sessions for the C-suite people. Some senior leaders didn't see the value of this work at all, while others couldn't understand how it wasn't glaringly obvious that it was needed.

What surprised those leading the engagement was that no matter how effective the organizational design, strategy, and team alignments are, it can all be derailed by a lack of leadership effectiveness. Leaders must have the capacity and capability to lead the new organization in the changing and complex business environment.

...

"I wanted to change the world. But I have found that the only thing one can be sure of changing is oneself."

—Aldous Huxley, English writer, novelist, and philosopher

These three examples have taught us that it's critical to change how change happens. To be effective at change, leaders have to work outside-in on the strategy and organizational alignment, inside-out on individual transitions and development, and with teams to get them to collaborate and increase their capacity to deal with more complex change in the future. But many leaders focus on only one of those areas and then wonder why change fails to achieve the desired results.

TOP FIVE WATCH-OUTS, TIPS, AND TRICKS

We've reviewed many different challenges and solutions to accelerating change in this book. Here we want to recap our top five watch-outs, tips, and tricks to help you ready yourself and your organization to apply the principles and tools you've learned.

Challenge #1: The Excitement of the Change Leader Is Good but Not Enough

This scenario is a common one. A senior leadership team feels the pain of the business's performance and wants to create a new product or service to increase revenue and dominate new markets. They discuss and swirl ideas among themselves for several months and arrive at a brilliant plan. They are excited about the new and enhanced strategy and direction to advance the company's products or services. Finally they are ready to "unveil" their work to the next level of leaders (who, in reality, will be the people charged with implementing the new big idea). The unveiling happens, and then nothing happens.

Tip #1: Allow People Time to Go through Their Own Process
Just because the leadership team has processed through the business challenges and arrived at a solution doesn't mean frontline leaders will be able to jump on board without their own processing. We have

seen many leaders who assume that their clarity of purpose will automatically translate to everyone else and magically create alignment with the new vision.

Change leaders need to honor other people's processes of learning and understanding. Allow people time to go through their own mental regimen to analyze the issues and think through solutions. Leaders can assist in the process by presenting a succinct business case for why the organization needs to change. Once the problem or opportunity is clearly outlined, leaders must focus on ensuring understanding, gaining commitment, and enabling action.

...

**"If you don't have time to do it right,
when will you have time to do it over?"**

—John Wooden, American basketball coach,
ten-time NCAA national champion

Challenge #2: The "One Great Mind" Syndrome

A smart, respected leader who works hard and means well develops a plan. The leader has a great idea, a strong will, and a high level of motivation to implement the change. He or she believes that on "one great mind" alone the organization will change.

Tip #2: No Involvement, No Commitment

"One great mind" isn't enough to solve the increasing demands of the business world and meet evolving stakeholder needs. Change leaders need to engage the heads, hands, and hearts of others in the organization to collaborate and solve new and complex problems.

Change leaders can create conditions for involvement and synergy, which include the following:

- A climate of openness and trust

- A skillful group process where all team members bring out the best in each other

- A strong level of commitment to the goal

- A clear understanding of the end in mind and result the team is after

- Clear measures of success and reporting processes

- A willingness to let go of past processes, practices, and solutions in favor of new and better ideas

...

"Good is the enemy of great. And that is one of the key reasons why we have so little that becomes great. We don't have great schools, principally because we have good schools. We don't have great government, principally because we have good government. Few people attain great lives, in large part because it is just so easy to settle for a good life."
—Jim Collins, American business consultant, author, and lecturer

Challenge #3: Do What I Say, Not What I Do

Senior leaders hire us to help them with a change initiative. As we interview various employee levels in the organization, we hear variations of these comments: "I hope while you're helping us to change you are also working with our leaders." Or, "I can't change anything until those above me change." We even hear remarks from senior leaders about the need to change the people or systems under them, clearly giving no thought to changing themselves.

Tip #3: Become an Expert in All Five Roles of Leaders

Do people have to wait for their leaders to change before they can change? No. We are all the masters of our own destiny. But what we have found over and over again is that employees look closely at senior leaders' behaviors, integrity, skills, motivations, and messages. Employees want to see their leaders "walking the talk." Leaders' congruence of message with behavior is the barometer employees use to gauge if they are serious about change. It's not that employees *can't* change without leaders changing first. Instead, it's that employees often *won't* change until they see behavioral evidence from leaders that a transformation is really happening.

Leading change means stepping in and being present by practicing the five roles of leaders:

- **Focus** the change effort and set a clear direction. Then repeat that direction over and over again until people can say it better than you can. Share what, why, when, and how change will happen every chance you get.

- **Align** the work of teams, functions, leaders, and employees to meet the needs of stakeholders and achieve business outcomes. Define and relentlessly measure the new behaviors required to be successful. Step in and define what is consistent or inconsistent with that focus in how processes, structures, and systems are designed and implemented.

- **Engage** people through communication, dialogue, and involvement to create the best solutions. Find out what is important to them and align their work to meet their interests and passion. Help employees get comfortable giving up what they are comfortable with now for something better in the future.

- **Lead** others as you want to be led. Create change champions throughout the business. Increase the collective leadership capacity by investing in the development of leaders (including yourself). Reward and promote leaders who exhibit an ability to get results and live the behaviors of the new culture.

- **Sustain** the change by staying involved in implementation to clear roadblocks, eliminate confusion, maintain priorities, and ensure stakeholder needs are met. To institutionalize change, enable employees to integrate new work and eliminate what's no longer needed.

...

"Action expresses priorities."

–Mahatma Gandhi, leader of Indian nationalism

Challenge #4: Inclination to Go Fast

Leaders are under pressure for various reasons to institutionalize an initiative. They realize the change will be somewhat messy and complex, so they believe speed is their best weapon against bogging down. Their mantra becomes "Let's move quickly and just get it done." They primarily use a top-down, outside-in approach. They hand down the "marching orders" and expect people to comply.

Tip #4: Spend Time on the "Soft" to Overcome the "Hard"

Leaders have to fight their inclination to "just get it done" and avoid the personal and emotional side of change that employees experience. Though it seems counterintuitive, going slow during change is the quickest path to improved results. Our clients in Asia seem to understand this instinctively. They spend time really understanding all issues and perspectives, then they work hard to get buy-in before moving to implementation. Western cultures tend to be more excited about the initial vision for change, but get bogged down during implementation because employees aren't on board. The combination of identifying the "hard" issues while also managing the "softer" emotional issues that employees wrestle with is the quickest way to success and long-term sustainability.

...

"Tell me and I forget. Teach me and I remember.
Involve me and I learn."

—Benjamin Franklin, one of the Founding Fathers of the United States

Challenge #5: Do More with the Same (or Less)

Leaders expect employees to keep the business running while at the same time defining and implementing the new work required by the change. Employees struggle to prioritize what's most important and to keep up with an ever-increasing workload.

Tip #5: Budget for More than You Think Is Needed

Constant prioritization and reallocation of time, energy, and resources is challenging. In fact, researchers have found that after an organization has introduced a new work process, behavior, or skill requirement, individuals and teams will have a dip in success and productivity while the new behavior is being "incorporated." This "Incorporation Effect" happens as people try to let go of their comfortable work and learn something new. Pushing through this period is critical to successful change. To ensure that changes are incorporated into the day-to-day work, leaders need to invest extra time, energy, and resources—between one and a half to two times more than they would initially estimate. The up-front time and cost to leaders is greater, but it pays off on the back end with fewer delays, better implementation, and faster results.

...

**"Success never comes without a price.
By the choices you make, you determine the cost."**

—Larry H. Miller, businessman and philanthropist

A SUMMARY OF HOW THIS APPROACH TO CHANGE IS DIFFERENT

As we conclude, let's summarize how this approach to change is different from that encouraged by other authors and practitioners in this field. Sir Winston Churchill said, "To improve is to change; to be perfect is to change often." Too many leaders change often—the organizational structure, the compensation system, the strategy. But great leaders transform their organizations, which requires them to fundamentally work differently from most leaders in three ways. First, they change how they think and talk about change. Second, they change their approach to change by engaging both individuals *and* the organization. And third, they elevate what they do as leaders and the roles they play.

1. Change How You Think and Talk about Change

Great leaders of change think and talk differently about change than do most leaders. They engage in Big Talk—conversations about the business that proactively explore sustainable improvements through wholesale change. Great change leaders discuss how to increase performance capacity, what needs to happen that is not currently happening, and what might prevent the organization from successfully implementing change. They don't postpone, passively approach, or even piecemeal change. Instead they proactively make change part of their ongoing leadership agenda.

2. Change Your Approach to Change

Great leaders approach change by engaging both individuals *and* the organization in change. For change to be sustainable, it *requires both an inside-out and an outside-in approach*. It *has to*. To change a team or business, you have to change both the thoughts and beliefs *and* the structure and systems. And to get it to stick, all levels of the organization have to be focused, aligned, and engaged in the same thing. Quick-fix changes don't work to improve long-term organizational health. To get lasting organizational improvements, great leaders create a culture that delivers lasting results. And that includes setting the direction, enabling processes and systems to work effectively, getting buy-in from employees, and "walking the talk." When all of these elements come together, change will happen at all levels.

3. Elevate Your Leadership

Great change leaders elevate what they do and the roles they play. Barack Obama, former president of the United States, said, "Change will not come if we wait for some other person or some other time. We are the ones we have been waiting for. We are the change that we have been seeking." Change can't be mandated; it must be modeled. Leadership is not a position; it's a role. Being an effective change leader requires self-awareness and improvement in all five roles that accelerate change—Focus, Align, Engage, Lead, and Sustain. Our experience has shown that leaders who play all five roles successfully transform their own performance as well as the results of their organizations.

A FINAL NOTE

Sydney Harris, journalist for the *Chicago Daily News* and the *Chicago Sun-Times*, observed, "Our dilemma is that we hate change and love it at the same time; what we really want is for things to remain the same but get better." The tough reality is that we know things won't get better without change. The art and elegance of leadership is to accelerate change and thereby accelerate getting better. Great change leaders deal with the emotional side of change. They allow people time to process, participate, and perform. They improve the organization by transforming teams. They constantly work to get better performance. They develop themselves and other leaders to ensure the business can handle current and future changes. These are the things leaders do to make things better.

Karen Kaiser Clark summarized the journey of change in this way: "Life is change. Growth is optional. Choose wisely." Opportunities await you and your organization. Establish focus, create alignment, encourage engagement, activate leadership, and ensure sustainability. It feels like a lot, but the alternative is to end up on the pile of hundreds of other failed change initiatives.

As you change the way you change, you'll experience personal and business results that far outweigh the price you pay. It's a wise choice that will ensure accelerated business performance.

THE COMPLEXITY AND SPEED OF CHANGE

"Everyone senses that business conditions are different from those of a few years ago, yet few grasp just how fundamental the changes are and how swiftly they are overtaking businesses of all kinds. The business environment has changed by an order of magnitude."

—Larry Bossidy and Ram Charan, authors of *Execution: The Discipline of Getting Things Done*

For years, all of us have read about and lived in a fast-changing world. The speed of change continues to accelerate. And yet, we have found that the complexity of change that leaders are facing is as difficult to deal with as the speed of change. The interplay between technology, workforce, and changing markets is difficult to navigate. To help leaders be aware of and begin to navigate the complexities the business is dealing with, one of our clients gathered the following findings from all different sources. We think these findings are helpful to starting conversations about change.

TECHNOLOGY CHANGES

- Email was the big collaboration buzzword twenty-five years ago, and many firms still predominantly rely on it for communicating, collaborating, and sharing.

- Today, 72% of companies are deploying at least one social software tool.

- In the next two years, organizations will increase their spending on enterprise social collaboration software at a compound annual growth rate of 61%.

- Multi-platform use is on the rise with 52% of online adults now using two or more social media sites.

CUSTOMER CHANGES

- 16% of customers have vented about negative customer service interactions through social channels.

- More than 68 million bloggers post reviews and recommendations about products and services.

- Twitter users are twice as likely to review or rate products online or visit company profiles as those who belong only to traditional social networking websites.

- 93% of marketers use social media for business.

INFORMATION CHANGES

- Every minute, seventy-two hours of video is uploaded to YouTube.

- Two billion people don't have a bank account, but they have a mobile phone (a primary financial enabler in emerging markets).

- Increasingly, organizations are using cloud technology to drive large-scale transformations. This includes enabling a flexible and mobile workforce (42%); improving alignment and interaction with customers, suppliers, and partners (37%); and leveraging data to improve business decisions (35%).

- By 2025, two to three billion more people will have Internet access.

DEMOGRAPHIC CHANGES

- In the next decade, 1.2 billion people will reach employment age—the largest number in history. Of these, 90% will be in developing and emerging markets.

- By 2025, 57% of the world's population will live in urban areas, up from 50% in 2010.

- Globally, the population over age sixty is projected to increase from just under eight hundred million today (11% of world population) to just over two billion in 2050 (22% of world population).

- For the world as a whole, life expectancy increased by two decades since 1950 (from forty-eight years in 1950–1955 to sixty-eight years in 2005–2010). During the current half century, the UN Population Division projects global life expectancy to rise further to seventy-six years.

- The share of older women (fifty-five-plus) remaining in the workforce has increased sharply over the past twenty years, from 23% in 1992 to 35% in 2012. Women are expected to account for 52% of the over-fifty-five workforce by 2022.

- By 2030, the global middle class will more than double to 4.9 billion. Rapid growth in China, India, Indonesia, Vietnam, Thailand, and Malaysia will cause Asia's share of the new middle class to more than double. Asia will host 64% of the global middle class and account for over 40% of global middle-class consumption.

ECONOMIC AND GEOGRAPHIC CHANGES

- China will overtake the United States to become the world's largest economy by 2020. China will be overtaken by India in 2050.

- Many economists expect growth in emerging markets to be four percentage points higher than growth in the first world countries for at least the next five years.

- Cities of the developing world will absorb roughly 95% of the total population growth expected worldwide in the next two decades, a result of rural to urban migration.

- Today there are three dozen megacities (ten-million-plus population) around the world, with the largest percentage in Asia. By 2030, more than a dozen will be added to the list.

CLIENT EXAMPLE OF PROJECT PHASES

n our change projects, we work with an eye toward sustainability. In every phase of the project, we build in activities to enable implementation. Included here is a phase gate approach to change created with one of our clients whose leaders tended to rush through the early stages of a project only to have to wait to get the commitment required from stakeholders in later stages. Following is a summary of key tasks by phase as well as the recommended deliverables that should be in place before moving on to the next phase of the project.

Key Tasks By Phase

	Assess	Scope & Select	Plan & Design
Phase Objective	Explore the opportunity/problem	Understand the approach needed to achieve desired results	Determine the steps to achieve desired results
Key things to consider to ensure success	Have you defined your initiative?	Have you defined your current to future state and identified the gap?	Do you have plans in place to address change impacts based on organizational factors?
	Have you identified all of your stakeholders and the impact of the change on them?	Do you have an approach to address the gaps? Have you defined your milestones and deliverables?	Do you have a plan prepared to execute?
	Have you clearly defined the case for change?	Have you defined how you will engage and communicate with your impacted stakeholders? Have you defined your key messages using the head, hands, and heart model?	Do you have your training plans in place to address skill gaps?
	Have you allocated the right resources to execute on this work and freed up the capacity to focus efforts?	Have you defined your skill gaps and identified how you will address them?	Are your materials developed and ready to support training requirements and close the skill gaps identified?
	Do you understand the impact on the organization that your initiative will have?	Are your leadership teams ready to model the change?	
	Have you obtained the right level of leadership approvals?	Have you defined key metrics for success?	
Don't move on until you've done these	• Determine business value and case for change • Assess alignment to business priorities • Align with sponsors	• Define scope, objectives, resources, outcomes, desired business impacts & behaviors, milestones, and KPIs	• Create detailed execution plans • Engage stakeholders • Prepare to address impacts to current business

Phase	Develop & Execute	Transition	Sustain & Close
Objective	Create the solution to deliver against the opportunity/problem	Implement the solution	Entrench the solution
Key things to consider to ensure success	Have you prepared your communications in advance?	Is your leadership team modeling the change?	Are you listening for issues, concerns, challenges, and risks and adjusting to alleviate?
	Have you executed your communications and engagement plans?	Are your stakeholders working in the desired future state? Have they changed behaviors?	Are you providing key information updates and support for your impacted stakeholders?
	Have you executed your training plans to build the right skills, knowledge, and reinforce future state behaviors?	Are sponsors of change ready to sustain the desired behaviors and business results?	Is your entire team modeling the change and working as expected in the future state? If not, do you need to adjust one or more of the organizational factors?
	Does your leadership team have the right information and support to model the changes?	Is ownership of this initiative ready to be transferred to the business unit? Are business owners committed and prepared to integrate this into the day-to-day operations?	Is there a process to capture lessons learned and best practices for continuous improvement?
	Do you have a plan in place to support and model the changes?	Are accountabilities in place and understood by the business?	Are business outcomes being measured and adjustments made?
	Do you have a plan in place to support the needs of your stakeholders after change is executed?	Has ownership of key metrics been transferred?	Are achievements regularly recognized and celebrated?
	Are sponsors prepared for change (model, communicate, drive, and execute)?		
Don't move on until you've done these	• Build and test solutions to meet requirements • Prepare stakeholder groups for change	• Ensure readiness for change and execute plans to meet project objectives • Stabilize after execution	• Assess metrics to ensure change is realized • Transition accountabilities

ACKNOWLEDGMENTS

The development of ideas, frameworks, tools, and stories that are the essence of this book have emerged from a cast of colleagues, partners, mentors, clients, and loved ones who've blessed our lives over the past twenty-five years working in this field. We stand on the shoulders of our extended community in our thinking, business practice, and writing about this body of work called leading change.

We have been taught and guided by some of the best mentors in the field of organization development, business strategy, business psychology, and management consulting. Those who have guided us include: Bill Adams, Norm Smallwood, Randy Stott, Vern Della-Piana, Jim Stuart, Stephen R. Covey, David Hannah, Stephen M. R. Covey, Steve Dichter, Barry Carden, Jim Hassinger, Rick Boyatzis, and Jonathan Spiegel.

We have also been challenged and inspired by colleagues. They have been at our side as we have had the privilege of teaching, coaching, and advising our clients in their most difficult (and sometimes most exciting) opportunities in their business life. Colleagues who deserve recognition include Troy Scotter, Ian Edwards, Dave Jennings, Tim Clark, Deb Hauck, Cathy Crosky, Neil Yeager, and John Beck. Special thanks and recognition to Lisa Daems, who challenged our thinking and edited our prose to make the writing clear and compelling. And to our colleagues at Greenleaf Book Group—thanks for seeing the potential of this book and working so collaboratively to make it a reality.

We deeply acknowledge our clients who have allowed us to partner with them over the years: Doug Guthrie at Comcast; John Mellott and Scott Whiteside at *The Atlantic Journal-Constitution*; Lisa Strogal at Cenovus Energy; Walt Bussels at Jacksonville Electric Authority; Chip Perry at TrueCar; David Leonard at UNC Executive Development; Kathy Parker at Endocyte; Neil Hunter at Suncor Energy; Catharyn Baird at The Ethics Game; Bill Cowley at Eli Lilly; and many other amazingly courageous clients. Your dedication, creativity, and discipline have been an honor to observe.

Finally, we have been supported and encouraged by our children, Nicole, Natalie, Josh, Timothy, and Morgan. Your love, feedback, patience, and kindness have been invaluable. Most of all we would like to acknowledge our respective spouses, Donna Lyman and Teresa Hargrave, for being both our greatest critics and our strongest advocates!

Bravo, and thanks to all.

NOTES

CHAPTER 1

1. Some of these questions are inspired by our friend Mahan Khalsa who wrote a great book called *Let's Get Real or Let's Not Play* (Portfolio, 2008). We love the title and think the idea is relevant to change efforts—leaders need to "Get Real" about the change they are proposing or employees will opt out and "Not Play."

2. Prosci Benchmarking Report, "Best Practices in Change Management," 2014 edition.

3. Ibid.

4. Ibid.

5. Peter Scholtes, *The Leader's Handbook: A Guide to Inspiring Your People and Managing The Daily Workflow* (New York: McGraw-Hill, 1997).

6. William Bridges, *Managing Transitions* (Boston: Addison Wesley, 1992), x.

7. Kerry Patterson et al., *Influencer: The New Science of Leading Change* (New York: McGraw-Hill, 2013), 28.

8. Dave Packard, "Industry's New Challenge: The Manager of Creativity," Western Electronic Manufacturers' Association, San Diego, September 23, 1964.

9. Robert M. Pirsig, *Zen and the Art of Motorcycle Maintenance* (New York: Bantam, 1975), 87–88.

10. Michael Hammer, quoted in "Washington Takes Leaf From Business Manuals," by Steve Lohr, *The New York Times*, September 8, 1993, http://www.nytimes.com/1993/09/08/us/washington-takes-leaf-from-business-manuals.html

11. Julie Gebauer and Don Lowman, *Closing the Engagement Gap: How Great Companies Unlock Employee Potential for Superior Results* (New York: Portfolio, 2008).

12. Maya Angelou, "Life's Work: An Interview with Maya Angelou," *Harvard Business Review* (May 2013), p. 152.

13. Robert J. Anderson and William A. Adams, *Mastering Leadership* (Boston: Wiley, 2015), 185, 181.

CHAPTER 2

1. Andrew S. Grove, *Only the Paranoid Survive: How to Exploit the Crisis Points that Challenge Every Company* (New York: Doubleday, 1996), 89.

2. BlessingWhite Study of 7,508 individuals from North America, India, Europe, and Southeast Asia including Australia and China, "The State of Employee Engagement 2008," p. 23.

3. Walter Kiechel, "Corporate Strategists Under Fire," *Fortune* (December 27, 1982), 38.

4. Chris McChesney, Sean Covey, and Jim Huling, *The 4 Disciplines of Execution* (New York: Simon and Schuster, 2012), Kindle edition, p. 5.

5. Ibid.

6. Ibid.

7. Ibid.

8. BlessingWhite Study of 7,508 individuals from North America, India, Europe, and Southeast Asia including Australia and China, "The State of Employee Engagement 2008," p. 1.

9. Used with permission.

10. Geoff Colvin, "Can Indra Nooyi Keep Investors Sweet on Pepsi?" *Fortune*, June 13, 2013, http://fortune.com/2013/06/13/can-indra-nooyi-keep-investors-sweet-on-pepsi

11. "Business Case for Change," A Cornerstone Group White Paper Series on Change, Shane R. Cragun, R. Kendall Lyman, Jim Dowling.

12. For more details, see Stephen J. Dubner, "What Do Hand-Washing and Financial Illiteracy Have in Common?" *Freakonomics Radio, New York Public Radio, (podcast)*, 2012.

13. Patrick Litre et al., "Results Delivery: Busting Three Common Myths of Change Management," Insights, Bain & Company, January 12, 2011.

14. Jay Finegan, "Four-Star Management," *Inc.* (January 1, 1987), http://www.inc.com/magazine/19870101/creech.html

15. McChesney, Covey, and Huling, *The 4 Disciplines of Execution,* 11.

16. Ibid., 12

17. Phil Jones, summary of Norton and Kaplan's study, Posted Nov 4, 2012 in 4G Balanced Scorecard, http://www.excitant.co.uk/2012/11/3629.html

18. McChesney, Covey, and Huling, *The 4 Disciplines of Execution,* 13.

19. Richard Rumelt, *Good Strategy, Bad Strategy,* iBooks, p. 85.

20. Phil Jones, summary of Norton and Kaplan's study, Posted Nov 4, 2012 in 4G Balanced Scorecard, http://www.excitant.co.uk/2012/11/3629.html

21. Richard Rumelt, *Good Strategy, Bad Strategy,* 85–86.

CHAPTER 3

1. Kerry Patterson et al., *Influencer,* 75.

2. Ibid., 76.

3. Tom Wujec, "Build a Tower, Build a Team," TED Talk, April 2010.

4. Alex "Sandy" Pentland, "The Hard Science of Teamwork," *HBR* Blog, 10:15 AM March 20, 2012.

5. Daniel Goleman, "Leadership that Gets Results," *Harvard Business Review,* March-April 2000, reprint R00204.

6. Thanks to our colleague Troy Scotter for this example.

7. Many scholarly articles have been written about the rationality in economic decision making and the cultural differences of different groups. We recommend an Internet search about the Ultimatum Game to better understand the methodology and findings.

8. ©Copyright Franklin Covey Co. All rights reserved. Used herein with permission. The OE Cycle is a model and methodology used by our colleagues at FranklinCovey. The version we use has been modified and refined over the years based on our work with clients. We're appreciative of our colleagues Dave Hanna, Jim Stuart, and Keith Gulledge and their original work in this area, and for their willingness to partner with us to design organizations using this approach.

9. Modified from FranklinCovey's OE Cycle Overview.

10. [From graphic] Anderson and Adams, *Mastering Leadership*, 202.

11. BlessingWhite, "The State of Employee Engagement 2008," p. 23.

12. Michael E. Porter, "What is Strategy?" *Harvard Business Review* (November-December 1996), 73.

CHAPTER 4

1. Timothy R. Clark, *Epic Change* (San Francisco: Jossey-Bass, 2008), 6.

2. "Effecting Change in Business Enterprises," New York: Conference Board, 2005, p. 18.

3. Kathleen D. Dannemiller is the originator of the DVF Change Formula sometimes erroneously attributed to Richard Beckhard who created a similar formula for overcoming resistance to change. The copyright of the DVF Change Formula is held by Dannemiller Tyson Associates and used by permission.

4. William Bridges, *Managing Transitions* (Reading, Mass: Addison-Wesley, 1991), 3–5.

5. Ibid., 5.

6. "The Emotional Cycle of Change" diagram is adapted from Elisabeth Kübler-Ross' "Five Stages of Death" from *On Death and Dying* Copyright © 1969 by The Elisabeth Kübler-Ross Family LP. Reprinted by arrangement with The Elisabeth Kübler-Ross Family LP and The Barbara Hogenson Agency. All rights reserved.

7. Patrick Litre et al., "Results Delivery," http://www.bain.com/publications/articles/results-delivery-busting-3-common-change-management-myths.aspx

8. Studies are aggregated from Towers-Watson, Hay Group, Gallup Organization, Hewitt Associates, and other smaller studies.

9. Jack Welch, *Business Week,* May 2006.

10. "The Global Workforce Study," Towers-Perrin, 2007.

11. Gebauer and Lowman, *Closing the Engagement Gap*, 9.

12. Hewitt Associates, "Percent of Organizations with Falling Engagement Scores Triples in Two Years," July 29, 2010, press release. "High engagement" firms are defined as those having 65% or more engaged employees. "Low engagement" firms feature less than 40% engaged.

13. Gallup meta-analysis of 199 research studies across 152 organizations in 44 industries and 26 countries covering 955,905 employees. J. Harter et al. (2009) "The Relationship Between Engagement at Work and Organizational Outcomes," Gallup Press.

14. Scott Flander, "Terms of Engagement," *Human Resource Executive*, January 1, 2008.

15. John Engen, "Are Your Employees Truly Engaged?" *Chief Executive*, March 2008.

16. Louis Gerstner, *Who Says Elephants Can't Dance?* (New York: HarperBusiness, 2003), 235.

CHAPTER 5

1. Louis Gerstner, *Who Says Elephants Can't Dance?* (New York: HarperBusiness, 2003), 11.

2. Ibid., 16.

3. Ibid., 15.

4. Charles Ferguson and Charles Morris, *Computer Wars: The Post-IBM World* (Frederick, MD: Beard Books, 1993).

5. Ibid.

6. Paul Carroll, *Big Blues: The Unmaking of IBM* (New York: Three Rivers Press, 1994), as quoted in Gerstner, *Who Says Elephants Can't Dance?*, 12–13.

7. Ibid., 37.

8. DDI, Global Leadership Forecast 2014/2015, http://www.ddiworld.com/DDI/media/trend-research/glf2014-findings/interacting-vs-managing_glf2014_ddi.pdf

9. E. Matson and L. Prusak, "Boosting the Productivity of Knowledge Workers," *McKinsey Quarterly*, 2010.

10.   We have adapted this idea to our change practice over the last fifteen years, based on our colleague Dee Groberg's original paper called "A Management vs. Leadership Approach to Change."

11.   Anderson and Adams, *Mastering Leadership*, 8.

12.   Dave Ulrich and Norm Smallwood, *Why the Bottom Line ISN'T!* (New York: Wiley, 2003), vii.

13.   Ibid., 1.

CHAPTER 6

1.   Kate Bonamici Flaim, "Winging It," *Fast Company* (October 1, 2007).

2.   Raphael Pustkowski, Jesse Scott, and Joseph Tesvic, "Why Implementa- tion Matters," http://www.mckinsey.com/insights/operations/why_ implementation matters

3.   John Kotter, *Leading Change* (Boston, MA: Harvard Business School Press, 1996).

4.   Gary Hamel and Michele Zanini, "Build a Change Platform, Not a Change Program," *McKinsey and Company Insights*, October 2014.

5.   Ibid.

6.   Alan Deutschman, *Change or Die* (New York: HarperCollins, 2007), 29.

7.   Our colleague Chris McChesney and his partners have done a masterful job detailing this concept given their experience with clients in their book *The 4 Disciplines of Execution*.

ABOUT THE AUTHORS

Kendall Lyman is a founding principal of The Highlands Group, a firm specializing in strategy, organizational change, and leadership development. He helps leaders around the world to navigate change, improve employee engagement, and transform culture.

He has consulted with a wide array of organizations ranging from Fortune 500 to small and midsize firms. He has worked across diverse industries such as oil and gas, lodging, government, and manufacturing. Kendall has consulted internationally on projects in Europe, Latin America, Asia, and Africa, and he speaks fluent Spanish. He has worked with senior leaders from Cenovus Energy, TrueCar, Lowe's, RentPath, Sun Life Financial, Endocyte, Autotrader.com, Suncor, Kellogg's, US Army Reserve, Eli Lilly, The National MS Society, US Navy, and The Atlanta Journal-Constitution.

Kendall's work with clients has been recognized nationally. The Navy Postal Group in Washington, D.C., won the Federal Mail Center Excellence Award; the Norfolk Naval Shipyard won the Virginia State Quality Award; and his participation in the work to split InterContinental Hotels Group from its parent company received the ASTD Excellence in Practice Award.

He has held executive line management responsibilities, including the Practice Leader of the Organizational Change Consulting Group at FranklinCovey. He began his career working in marketing and sales at IBM. Kendall is co-author of the management series *The Business Strategy Audit*, the white paper series *A Case for Change Management*, and the book *The Employee Engagement Mindset*.

Kendall lives with his wife and three children in the Salt Lake City, Utah, area. He holds an MBA from Brigham Young University.

...

Tony C. Daloisio, Ph.D., is a principal of The Highlands Group and founder/CEO of the Charter Oak Consulting Group (one of *Inc.* magazine's fastest growing privately held firms; see www.cocg.com). Tony earned a BA and Ph.D. in Psychology and Education from the University of Connecticut, and an MA in Counseling Psychology from Fairfield University.

The first ten years of Tony's career were spent in Education as a teacher, counselor, and inner city public high school leader, and as the executive director of the Yale University Child Study Lab School for Emotionally Disturbed Youth. In the mid 1980s, Tony made the decision to move into the world of business where he became vice president of Human Resources for MassMutual Financial Services. In the mid 1990s for 5 years, he was retained by McKinsey & Company to co-lead the design of their change management practice. While at McKinsey, in addition to his work in developing the change management approach, he led McKinsey consulting teams focused on change management and the effective implementation of strategic imperatives with many Fortune 100 firms in the world. In early 2000, he was retained by FranklinCovey to create its Principle-Centered Change practice and to lead large-scale change projects for senior teams. In addition to consulting in change management, Tony led the Center for Creative Leadership's flagship leadership development program, and he was a lead faculty member in the innovative Master's in Management program offered by the American Management Association.

Tony's current focus is on consulting with CEOs and their teams to build capability, implement strategy, and support major change. He has extensive experience coaching senior executives and executive teams to effectively transform their business. He has worked with leaders from Emory University Health Care, New York Life, the US

Social Security Administration, The Ladders, Accenture, The Atlanta Journal Constitution, Bain Consulting, the US Navy, McKinsey & Company, Comcast, Mercedes-Benz, Autotrader.com, United Business Media, and Lowe's.

Residing in both Atlanta, GA, and Washington Depot, CT, Tony is married to Teresa Hargrave. They have two children and two grandchildren.

ABOUT OUR CONSULTING PRACTICE

The Highlands Group is a management consulting firm that specializes in strengthening individual, team, and organizational performance. We partner with client organizations to accelerate their ability to improve business performance. We work with a wide variety of clients including Government, Fortune 500 companies, and not-for-profit organizations.

Kendall and Tony have partnered in delivering business solutions for the past 15 years. They pride themselves in approaching consulting, leadership team development, and executive team coaching in a customized, practical, results-oriented, and highly engaging manner. Key offerings include the following:

1. **Consulting Projects**: Organizational diagnosis, strategy formulation and execution, process alignment and improvement, and cultural transformation.

2. **Executive Education**: Design and delivery of executive leadership development programs for leaders around the world.

3. **C-suite Team Development**: Leadership team capability building in areas such as organization alignment, leading change, working together effectively, and building collective leadership capacity.

4. **Executive Coaching**: One-on-one coaching to enhance individual leadership effectiveness in assigned accountabilities.

5. **Employee Engagement**: Engagement surveys, instructor-led workshops, personal coaching, and organizational engagement consulting projects.

6. **Change Management**. Enabling change through change courses (Leading People through Change, Making Change Happen), executive coaching for leaders experiencing change, change consulting oversight including change strategy, managing the change process, and senior leader support.

7. **Keynote Speeches**: Topics include change management, leadership effectiveness, and employee engagement.

8. **Team Retreats**: Custom design and facilitation of team retreats.

For the latest about change, please visit us at www.changethewayyouchange.com. For a more detailed description of our offerings, clients, industries, and contact information, please visit our website at www.highlandsgrp.com.

INDEX

L

La Fontaine, Jean De, 33
lag measures, 48–50, 199
Lao Tzu, 166
Lawrence, D. H., 15
lead measures, 48–50, 199
Lead role, 19
leaders. *See also* leadership
    budgeting by, 215
    changing approach to change,
      217
    changing themselves, 212–15
    characteristics of, 147–48
    developing self and others,
      168–171
    encouragement of employees
      engagement in change by, 8
    inclination to go fast, 214–15
    increasing collective capacity of,
      viii
    identifying stage they are in in
      emotional cycle, 122
    integrity and quality of, 164–68
    lack of trust in, 155
    leading change process, 152–54
    more needed than, 210–12
    prioritizing by, 215
    relationships with others, 143–44
    removal of restraining barriers by,
      155–159
    roles of, 17–20
    self-awareness by, 20
    thinking and talking about
      change, 216
leader's shadow, 164–68

leadership, 205–18. *See also* leaders
    client case examples, 206–9
    in Diagnosis Cycle, 94
    IBM example, 140–42
    lack of, 7
    vs. management approach to
      change, 149–51
    newspaper business example,
      144–47
    overview, 205–6
    as role, not position, 217
    strength of, 163
leadership spine, 159–64
Lean manufacturing, 73–74
learning
    as engagement driver, 133–34
    establishing, 199–202
LeBlanc, Chase, 150
levels of change, 14–16
Lewis, C. S., 120
light plans, 60, 62f
Lincoln, Abraham, 55
Lindbergh, Anne Morrow, 134
Lombardi, Vince, 171
Lyman, Kendall, ix, x, 128, 140,
    145, 235

M

Machiavelli, Niccolo, 3
Mahfouz, Naguib, 23
management approach to change, vs.
    leadership, 140–51
Managing Transitions (Bridges), 185
Mandela, Nelson, 199